Rising Soul

Rising Soul

A Guide To Personal Development

2nd Edition
By Dr. Muhammad Mansur

Translated & Adapted By
MAS Youth

ACTIVISM · SPIRITUALITY

MAS YOUTH

TARBIYAH

2008

MAS Publications
Falls Church, Va.
www.masyouth.org

Published by MAS Publications, Falls Church, VA
In cooperation with MAS Youth
First edition published 2007. Second edition 2008.

Cover design by Zaid Hisham.
Cover illustration by Aisha Hyder.
Interior design by Michael Dyer
Printed in the U.S.A.

ISBN 978-0-9792113-0-0

MAS Youth moves young people to strive for social justice and God-consciousness and convey Islam with utmost clarity.

Special thanks to the MAS Youth editing
teams that worked on this project.

*May Allah count this on
their scales of good deeds.*

Contents

A Word from MAS Youth

It is my honor and pleasure to introduce the first book published by MAS Youth. This milestone couldn't come at a better time, and the selection of the book couldn't be more adequate.

Several years ago, MAS Youth, the youth division of the Muslim American Society[1], emerged from a challenging transition that affected all of MAS. We are now witnessing the beginning of the harvest season, as MAS Youth grows and expands in many different directions. This success is attributed first to Allah (swt) and then to a nobility of mission and soundness of methodology, both prophetic in nature and deeply rooted in the Quran.

MAS realizes that self-reform and character development are a cornerstone of Islam and the methodology of the Quran and the Messenger. Allah praised the Prophet's manners in the Quran: ⟨Verily you are of great character⟩ and Prophet Muhammad summarized his mission by saying, "I have been sent to perfect human character." This unique feature in the MAS approach, combined with an emphasis on collective and organized work, is our most effective tool in our mission to rekindle the faith, organize and mobilize the community of believers, and put the Divine guidance to work in the service of the greater good for all humanity.

The young reader should approach this book intending to go through the same, soul-shaking transformation that the companions of Prophet Muhammad went through. In addition to reading the book, we invite you to learn more about MAS and explore its approach to self-development and reform.

Dr. Souheil Ghannouchi
MAS Executive Director
October 12, 2006

1 To learn more about the Muslim American Society (MAS) and its methodology, see the Afterword by MAS President Dr. Esam Omeish.

Often I hear young activists use the word tarbiyah. When I ask them "what do you mean?" the answer is unsure.

This translation was born in response to the widespread use of the word tarbiyah on the scene of Islamic activism, without a clear definition of its purpose and methods. This book is a simple, comprehensive guide to the self-development process of tarbiyah. It explains that tarbiyah is a continuous process that starts on the day we are born and ends the day we die. The aim of this process is to develop oneself to be a better and more God-conscious citizen.

Tarbiyah is a personal responsibility. However, there is a great role for mentors in helping individuals apply it to themselves. MAS employs tarbiyah as its core methodology, and through the MAS Youth Usra Program, MAS Youth provides mentors to guide young activists in their quest of achieving God-consciousness.

I ask Allah (swt) to accept this work—for MAS Youth seeks nothing but the reward of Allah. We ask Him to continue to utilize us to serve His cause and contribute to humanity by living and conveying the message He sent to us through the final messenger, Muhammad, peace be upon him.

Hazem Said
MAS Youth President
October 12, 2006

Introduction

Activism and spirituality symbolize the wings by which those yearning for Allah seek flight. Nevertheless, if one is going to soar, he must ensure that both wings are functioning and operating together as a cohesive unit. Muslims in Western countries struggle to attain this balance and, in some cases, have fallen into one of two extremes: monasticism or materialism.

The former is denounced by Allah who says, ⟨But the monasticism which they invented for themselves, We did not prescribe for them: We commanded only seeking the good pleasure of Allah.⟩² At the same time the fragile reality of the material world is exposed by the Quran. Men and women of understanding are challenged to see through the futility of its promises:

⟨ *The likeness of the life of the present is as the rain which We send down from the skies. By its mingling arises the produce of the earth, which provides food for men and animals. It grows till the earth is clad with its golden ornaments and is decked out in beauty—the people to whom it belongs think they have all powers of disposal over it. Then reaches it Our command by night or by day, and We make it like a harvest clean-mown, as if it had never flourished.⟩ ³*

Therefore, the true believer is not one who shuns the worldly life, but addresses it. He does not surrender to its pleasures, but controls them. For that reason Imam Ahmad was asked if a person who possessed 100,000 dirhams could be an ascetic. His response was, "As long as the money is in his hand and not his heart."

As Muslims wrestle with the articulation of Islam in the Western context, it is important to realize that Islamic spirituality has certain

2 The Quran, 57:27.
3 The Quran, 10:24.

qualities which distinguish it and make it unique. Let us take some time to focus on some of them.

1. *Comprehensive.* The program of spiritual exercise set out by Islam does not merely address one aspect of human existence. Rather, it seeks to touch upon all aspects of life: spiritual, physical, individual, and social. The relationship with Allah carries over into one's daily life, improving it; creating a person who is a better father, mother, coworker and citizen. It is not a process that solely focuses on a few spiritual exercises. Rather, one's ability to interact and bring benefit to his community represents the brightest ray that shines from an illuminated heart. This comprehensive understanding is mentioned by Allah (swt) when He describes the objectives of Prophethood:

> ❴ We have sent among you a Messenger of your own, rehearsing to you Our Signs, purifying you, and instructing you in Scripture and Wisdom, and in what you did not know. ❵ [4]

Commenting on the statement, "And purifying you" Ibn Kathir explained, "Purifying you from corrupt morals, the impurities of the soul and foolish actions." [5]

2. *Practical.* Although one will find challenges on the way towards building and maintaining one's spiritual state, there should be nothing on this path that makes attaining this relationship impossible. Referring to this Allah (swt) says, ❴ Allah desires ease for you, and He does not desire for you difficulty. ❵ [6] And, ❴ Allah desires that He should make light your burdens, and man is created weak. ❵ [7]

For this reason, it is sad to see some falling into acts of radicalism and deviance when seeking the spiritual path. Unnecessary burdens, extreme acts of hardship, exaggerated infatuations with technicali-

4 The Quran, 2:151.
5 Tafsir Ibn Kathir.
6 The Quran, 2:185.
7 The Quran, 4:28.

ties, and complete ignorance of the human condition do not represent the true divine teachings. In fact, the Prophet✲ always kept things in the realm of the plausible and encouraged his followers to do the same. Aishah, may Allah be pleased with her, narrates, "Whenever Allah's Apostle ordered the Muslims to do something, he used to order them to perform deeds which were easy for them to do, according to their endurance."[8]

3. *Contemporary.* If one were to glance at the large number of books and CD covers, advertisements for conferences and lectures in the West, one would be hard-pressed to find an image that does not reflect some aspect of our historical past. Although familiarity with one's past is the means to developing a healthy future, I would like to see Muslims going to work with a skyscraper backdrop, mothers taking children to school or a group of young Muslims playing football.

Our past has become opium. A means, if you will, of not dealing with the present. Although we can revel in our historical glory, the realities of making it to work or school on time, raising young children and functioning in a trans-modern world will not go away. Allah (swt) completed our faith, perfected it, and sent the Prophet✲ as a continuous mercy for the ages. The method of spirituality employed by our faith enables us to address and meet the realities of the daily grind. Racing to work, suffering through finals, and the hardships of present-day life are easily addressed through the works and thoughts of contemporary scholars. Thus, it is important for Muslims, while maintaining an important bond with their historical legacy, to contextualize their spiritual aims with the reality of life that they live in.

The work before you represents an important contribution towards achieving the above mentioned points. The author simplified the process of spiritual purification and centered it around two important principles: sound knowledge and sound practice. It is

8 Sahih Al-Bukhari Volume 1, Book 2, Number 19.

hoped that this work will quench the thirst that many of our young Muslim brothers and sisters in the West have for drawing nearer to Allah. I would like to congratulate the translator of this important work and pray that Allah will continue to bless her, her husband and their daughter.

MAS Youth presents this book as a gift to the many young and old who have experienced an awakening in recent years. It is our hope that the new generations of Muslims in the West will be able to present a clear, balanced and beneficial message to their fellow citizens. I pray that Allah will bless those who read this book, make it a proof for them and allow us to drink from the blessed hands of the Prophetﷺ.

One in need of Allah's mercy,
Suhaib D. Webb
October 12, 2006

Rising Soul

Part I
Abandoning Negative Habits

Every human being is created with a mix of positive and negative tendencies, so that Allah can test our commitment to self-purification. As we begin this journey of self-development, it is important to remember not to become frustrated. There are some negative characteristics that will cling to us relentlessly and will require persistent effort. We may never be able to remove a quick temper from our personality, but we can control it and prevent it from harming others. We can also learn methods to limit our susceptibility to the whispers of shaitan[1] who attacks our hearts at their weakest points.

In order to abandon our immoral habits, we first must discover what those habits are. The process of development and purification begins with self-examination. What areas do I need to work on? How can I allow my soul to rise higher and higher, away from what is wrong and closer to what Allah loves? A young Muslim can identify the areas she must work on by spending time assessing and evaluating her own behavior. She can study and interact with people around her, observing them and searching for similarities in her own character.

---

1 The Arabic name for the devil or satan. In Islam, every individual is held accountable for his own actions; the whisperings of satan are no excuse to be led astray.

Finally, it is essential that the young Muslim searches for a group of righteous, sincere friends and mentors who will help him grow closer to Allah, give him feedback on his weaknesses, and advise him well when he needs guidance. Umar ibn Al-Khattab, a great companion of the Prophet, once said, "May Allah have mercy on the one who points out to me a fault in my character."

Seeking Admiration

Study this chapter and examine your heart. Learn to identify the warning signs of riya', or seeking admiration. It is one of the major pitfalls for Muslims, young and old, whether inexperienced or devout. While the struggle against riya' is continuous and difficult, through it we can join the company of those engaged in jihad[1] and self-purification. Through it, we can gain a firmer grip on sincerity and pure intentions, essential elements required to obtain the pleasure of Allah.

What is Riya'?

The young Muslim who is afflicted with riya' displays his good actions in order to earn the admiration and praise of others. Searching for approval, such an individual longs for his acts of worship to be seen by people. Riya' can also be translated as showing off, hypocrisy, and insincerity. Allah warns strongly against riya' in the Quran: ❪So woe to the worshippers, who are neglectful of their prayers: those who only want to be seen [yura'un].❫[2]

---

1 Jihad literally means struggle. Jihad refers to the internal struggle for self-purification as well as the material struggle for justice, peace, and inviting to Islam.
2 The Quran, 107:4-6.

The Prophet♎[3] also cautioned against this affliction,

> Allah says: I am completely independent of any partner. Whoever does an action, intending my pleasure and the pleasure of another, the action will be left to the other. I am free of such an action.[4]

Riya' can affect the heart of any believer, no matter how long they have been practicing and no matter how devout they may appear. It creeps upon the Muslim like the silent footsteps of a tiny insect; seeking help from Allah and constant watchfulness are the best safeguards.

The Different Forms of Riya'

Riya' can take various forms in the heart of a Muslim. There is explicit riya', which manifests itself in speech or actions. A Muslim who suffers from explicit riya' in his speech may speak righteous, inspiring words within the earshot of people, hoping to draw out their praise and admiration. He may overtly move his lips in dhikr[5] so that someone notices his devotion. Perhaps he gives constructive, Islamic advice to a friend, but wishes secretly that people would be impressed by his piety and sound judgment. He may avidly seek knowledge so that others praise his dedication and wisdom.

This explicit form of riya' will also appear in actions. A Muslim might display extra devotion in her prayer so that people admire her concentration and piety. She might secretly hope that someone is watching her when she drops money in a donation box. If the young Muslim suffers from riya' in her actions, she might find herself working

3 This Arabic notation signifies the phrase Salla Allahu Alaihi wa sallam: peace be upon him. Muslims pronounce this phrase whenever the Prophet's name is mentioned.
4 Narrated by Imam Muslim.
5 The remembrance of Allah.

tirelessly in the name of Islam, but for the sake of her own ego; so that she might be admired as sincere, devout, and hardworking. With minimal self-examination, these explicit types of riya', both in speech and action, are easily identifiable.

Hidden riya' is of quite a different nature, one we should constantly scrutinize and guard against. It is a subtle, concealed form that is more difficult to detect than the footsteps of an ant, as the Prophetﷺ described it. Strive to cleanse any traces of this hidden riya' from your heart. This riya' is ever so slight, but it can make your good deeds worthless. In order to detect it, you must spend time in deep reflection, prayer, and self-examination. Because this riya' is so concealed within the self, the Prophetﷺ taught us to say,

> O Allah! We seek your protection from associating partners with you knowingly, and we ask Your forgiveness for doing so unknowingly.[6]

Learn this dua[7] and recite it often. There are also some signs to look for that may indicate hidden riya' creeping into your heart. Some of these indications follow.

You may find yourself dragging your feet and feeling reluctant to perform a good deed, until someone is watching you. Then, it suddenly feels easier and less burdensome. Or perhaps you feel glad that someone witnessed you performing a good deed, or love it when people admire your actions. While they notice you, you find yourself basking in their congratulations. When the praise dies down, you may find that continuing those good actions has become a heavy task.

Another indication that hidden riya' may have crept into your heart is overly fearing people's criticism. A coward standing amongst brave soldiers will not run, even if his intention is weak, lest he be condemned for his lack of courage.

6 Narrated by Ahmad.
7 Dua is a supplication: the act of calling upon Allah.

A Warning to Young, Active Muslims

After learning of the graveness of the sin and the stealth of riya', it might cross your mind that it is better to steer clear of doing anything in front of anybody. You may feel paralyzed and afraid to do any good deed in public, lest you fall into riya'. Watch out! If this has occurred to you, you have encountered precisely the trap that shaitan has laid for the believers.

The ultimate objective of shaitan is to drive you away from doing good deeds. He will try any method and use every deception, whether busying you with the stress of your daily life or manipulating your understanding of your religion, in order to decrease the net amount of good deeds you accumulate. One of his methods is to convince a sincere, striving Muslim that, because she is pious, she should not do good deeds in front of people. By doing so, he decreases the net amount of good deeds this young person will perform, since a great deal of her time is spent in the presence of others.

Instead of listening to these whisperings, you should race to perform good deeds no matter who is watching you. Allah does not want us to halt our journey of self-improvement because someone is observing—He wants us to serve Him regardless of the circumstances. Just to spite the shaitan, perform those deeds with a renewed burst of enthusiasm. It should not matter whether you are in the presence of many or are the only, solitary soul left on earth. Frustrate the shaitan and prove that his whisperings are futile. Your commitment to working for Allah, in public and in private, cannot be disrupted.

What is *not Riya'*

The following are symptoms that you may mistake as riya'. However, they are in fact positive actions and mindsets that are signs of dedication to goodness and calling to Allah.

1. *Setting an Example.* Displaying your actions with a clear intention of inspiring others to follow your example is not riya'. In fact,

your reward increases twofold, as you are engaging in jihad against the whisperings of riya' and also pursuing the reward of dawah[8] for the sake of Allah through your actions. However, only the Muslim who is confident in her intention should set an example through action. Her sincerity and intentions should be resolute. In her mind, what people think of her is insignificant—whether they are praising or criticizing makes no difference to her. She performs her worship and good deeds as if she were the only soul left on earth, watched by none but the Creator.

If your conviction is not at this level, and you cannot be sure that you will disregard the admiration, then neither seek out public actions nor stop yourself from performing them if someone happens to be watching. Focus inward and concentrate on the state of your own heart, regardless of where you are or who surrounds you.

2. *Committing a sin secretly,* fearing that people might see you. Sometimes, we look over our shoulder when we commit a sin, fearing what people would think if they saw us. Thus, instead of seeking out admiration for good deeds, we fear attention to our bad deeds. This is not riya'. The shame you feel is the tug of conscience and your fitra[9] deep inside you. The fact that no one learned of your sin is the grace of Allah, covering and hiding the faults of His servants.

3. *Feeling motivated and energized* in the presence of righteous friends. This too is not riya', even if you feel your level of inspiration decline when you leave a group of friends who remember Allah. As long as your intentions remain pure, and your motivation revolves around working for the pleasure of Allah, this rush you experienced

---

8 Dawah literally means an invitation. It refers to the great
  mission of inviting others to Allah and the religion of Islam.
9 The natural, pure state existing in every human
  being, which recognizes God and is drawn to Him.

is why Allah commandèd in the Quran, ⟨Help one another in righteousness and piety.⟩[10]

Your brother in Islam is a source of strength and motivation; take advantage of his companionship by encouraging one another to remember Allah and serve Him. That is what brotherhood and sisterhood in Islam are for.

Degrees of Riya'

The following descriptions are examples of different degrees of riya', which correspond to varying degrees of punishment.

1. *Completely disregarding Allah's reward*, seeking only the approval of people. An example is someone who only prays among her friends, and neglects her prayer when she is by herself at home. This is the worst kind of riya' and is a great sin in front of Allah.

2. *Intending primarily to show off* or win acceptance, with a secondary intention for reward. This person will also slacken when she is alone, since the intention for reward is more of an afterthought. This is similar to the first kind of riya', and its punishment is similar.

3. *Seeking both reward and admiration* with the same intensity. Whatever good this person does is negated by riya'. This person may also be accumulating sins with his mixed intentions. We have already mentioned the hadith[11] of the Prophet☷: "Allah says: I am the most independent of any partner…" This hadith indicates that the one who commits riya' has committed a grave sin that is almost as ominous as shirk[12], even when the intentions of reward and showing off are equal.

---

10 The Quran, 5:2.
11 A hadith is a saying of Prophet Muhammad☷. The sayings of Prophet Muhammad were meticulously documented and recorded during and after his death.
12 Associating partners with Allah.

4. *Feeling encouraged* by the admiration and presence of people. Knowing that an audience is watching them makes the performance of good deeds easier and more enjoyable to some Muslims. However, when people are not watching, these Muslims will not abandon those deeds. It is believed that they will be rewarded according to however strongly they pursued the reward of Allah, and will be punished according to how eagerly they sought the approval of people. In other words, their reward will be proportionate to the amount of sincerity, and their punishment will correspond to the amount of riya'.

How Riya' is Judged by Allah

The action that is performed outright for the sake of earning someone's admiration or approval is rejected by Allah. It is nullified, and sins take its place on the scale of this Muslim. He will get nothing for that good deed except grief, wasted effort, and punishment.

An initial action begun with the intention of pleasing Allah, but later overtaken by riya', will be judged by Allah in his wisdom. If you battled against the whisperings of riya' and eventually defeated them, you will be rewarded. Your reward will be for striving to improve yourself in addition to that of the original intended action. However, if you succumb to riya', then it is hoped that you will be rewarded for whatever part of that action was meant for Allah. You will receive no reward for what was spoiled with false intentions, and will instead taste punishment.

Let us assume that you performed an action purely for the sake of Allah, but later told people about it or felt happy when people discovered what you did. The judgment of this action depends on the circumstances: If your intention in informing people was to deliberately win their acceptance and admiration, then the action is not rejected, but the reward decreases to the extent of the corrupt intention. This may continue to the point that all reward is lost and sins begin to accumulate. We hope that repentance after every action would compensate for any decrease in our reward because of mixed intentions.

If you were pleased when people found out about a noble action, the action is not nullified nor is the reward decreased, as long as you did not intentionally seek their praise. You should not be excited that people are admiring you. Rather, you are hopeful that Allah is showing you a sign that your action was accepted.

The Prophet☵ was asked, "Messenger of Allah, what happens to a man who does a good deed, and then people praise him for it?"

"These are the glad tidings for the believer," answered the Prophet.[13]

How Can I Fight Against Riya'?

After learning of the nature of riya', its danger and disguises, we can now turn to the solution. The remedy for any illness of the heart is both knowledge and action.

1. *Knowledge.* If you suspect that riya' resides in your heart, know that it is lethal and leads to severe punishment in the Hereafter. Realize that the anxiety and stress that comes with worrying about what people think of you is a sickness brought about by riya'. The admiration of people is a goal that can never be truly reached, for as soon as one group approves of you, another scorns you. Even if people finally accept you, it is possible that respect will turn overnight into contempt.

Know that Allah is the Only One whose pleasure is worth working for and sweating for. Only with Him can you find complete solace, peace of mind, acceptance, mercy, and salvation. When someone truly knows and internalizes this knowledge, rooting it in his convictions, the temptation of riya' will become weaker.

13 Muslim.

2. *Action*. The Muslim who fears riya' must act! Study your heart, learn what affects change in yourself, and take all possible measures to cure the disease. These measures can include persistence in battling and reforming the frame of mind that leads to riya'. Time spent in solitary worship may accustom your heart to feeling alone before Allah. Seek refuge in Allah from the whisperings of shaitan and the temptation of running after others' approval and acceptance. Remind yourself often of the punishment of someone who gives in to riya'. Another measure is to keep your actions inconspicuous when possible and avoid mentioning it after it is performed.

These steps are difficult at first, and you may find yourself in a head-to-head struggle with your own desires and weaknesses. However if you are determined to purify yourself, Allah will help you to fight off riya' when it comes near you. He says in the Quran, ⟨Verily Allah does not change the condition of a people until they change what is in their hearts.⟩[14]

By taking the sincere, committed initiative to change the state of your heart, Allah will be there to help you change your condition.

---

14 The Quran, 13:11.

Backbiting

Islam fosters respect and brotherhood between all human beings. Any contempt, feelings of superiority, or ridicule for another human being is completely out of line with Islamic principles: principles such as the equality of all people and the susceptibility of every individual to mistakes. The prevalence of a habit such as backbiting does not detract from its evil.

Gheebah, backbiting or gossip, is to say something about your brother in his absence that he would dislike. Gheebah can also be any gesture that is meant to demean someone, such as rolling eyes, mocking someone when their attention is diverted, writing about someone, or anything similar. Allah says in the Quran,

> *And do not backbite one another. Would one of you like to eat the flesh of his dead brother? You would abhor that!* [1]

The Prophetﷺ once asked his companions, "Do you know what gheebah is?"

"Allah and His Messenger know best."

"It is to mention your brother in a way that he would not like," said the Prophet.

1 The Quran, 49:12.

One of the companions asked, "What if what we say about our brother is true?"

"If it is true, you have committed gheebah. If it is false, you have slandered him!" the Prophet said.[2]

The worst form of backbiting is to praise oneself indirectly by demeaning another. In other words, you backbite about someone else in order to make yourself look and feel good in comparison to whoever you are talking about. Another evil form of this habit is to pretend to have good intentions toward someone, while you are actually trying to debase and expose her while she is absent. One might say, "Did you know that so and so talks back to her parents and argues with them everyday? Let's pray that Allah guides her to what is right and teaches her good manners!" Veiling backbiting with a righteous supplication does not change the nature of the talk. It is also dangerous to gossip about a group of people, since the punishment may be multiplied. The Muslim who listens to someone else gossiping shares in the sin, because he is accepting the act implicitly through his silence. If you are listening to a conversation and gossip is taking place, you can avoid sharing in the sin by responding with the following actions:

1. Stop the backbiting immediately in its tracks by speaking up in defense of your brother or sister!

2. If it is impossible for you to speak up, then change the subject.

3. If you are unable to redirect the conversation, get up and leave.

4. If all of this is still impossible, then condemn the backbiting in your heart.

---

2 Narrated by Muslim.

The Messengerﷺ said, "Whoever defends the reputation of his brother, Allah will defend him from the Hell-fire on the Day of Judgment."[3]

Suspicion is a Form of Gheebah

> ❴ O you who believe! Avoid suspicion as much as possible, for suspicion in some cases is a sin. And do not spy on others, nor gossip behind their backs. Would any of you like to eat the flesh of his dead brother? You would abhor it...But fear Allah: For Allah is Oft-Returning, Most Merciful. ❵[4]

Suspicion is wrong when firmly rooted in the heart in the absence of clear proof. Such suspicion inevitably leads to wrongful action, such as resentment or giving someone the cold shoulder. This sinful suspicion is actually a kind of gheebah that resides in the heart, and is not always manifested in speech like gossip. As for passing thoughts and fleeting doubts about your brother or sister, this suspicion is not sinful. It will be forgiven, insha'allah, provided that you immediately dismiss the doubts so they do not translate into actions or bad feelings.

If you have seen your brother do something inexcusable with your own eyes, and resent his actions in your heart, then this is not suspicion. It is backed by real, undeniable proof. However, it is not permissible to spy on your brother, seeking to unearth the faults that he tries to hide from you. Spying on another person is strictly forbidden, as Allah says, ❴ And do not spy... ❵[5]

If you ever feel suspicious or resentful towards a Muslim, then immediately make sincere, persistent dua for her. Such a response will spite shaitan and dispel the doubt from your mind. Even if a trustworthy Muslim relates something about another Muslim, beware of your

3 Narrated by Tirmidhi.
4 The Quran, 49:12.
5 Ibid.

heart turning against your sister due to mere rumor and speculation. It may be possible the individual may have made a mistake or misunderstood. Perhaps your sister whom you doubt has an excuse for her actions, or has repented sincerely to Allah for her mistake. You did not witness anything yourself, so keep your heart clean of all suspicion towards brothers and sisters in Islam.

If your brother performs an unmistakable offense before your own eyes, you do not have the right to condemn or expose him. Instead, your response should be measured, caring, and controlled. Advise him gently, in secret and without exposing him. Ibn Masud, may Allah be pleased with him, said, "We were forbidden from spying, but if something happened in front of us, we acknowledged it." A just Muslim responds to this situation with kind advice and real concern. He reminds his brother of the punishment of the fire and the pleasure of pleasing Allah.

Is Gheebah Ever Allowed?

There are a few, rare circumstances in which talking about someone behind his or her back is excused. They are limited to the following situations.

1. *Speaking out against an oppressor.* Those who are oppressed or wronged can mention their complaints and accusations to the party who will grant them their right, such as a judge or other authority.

2. *When seeking a fatwa[6].* If you ask a learned person about someone's actions, in order to obtain a solution or a ruling, mentioning the person's deeds would be permissible. Hind bint Utbah asked the Prophet, "Abu Sufyan [her husband] is stingy and does not give me or my children what we need. Can I take from his money without his permission?" The Prophet replied, "You can take what you and

---

6 A religious ruling pertaining to a specific situation.

your children need, within just limits."[7] Thus, the companion mentioned that her husband was stingy, and the Prophet did not admonish her for gossiping since she was seeking advice from him. However, it would be better not to identify the individual and describe the situation in a general way.

3. *When warning others.* This would apply, for example, in a situation where someone is seeking a marriage partner. If you are asked to recommend someone for marriage, it is necessary that you disclose what you know about a brother or sister. However, this information should be revealed confidentially, with the intention of offering good advice, not to humiliate and create rifts. A similar situation would be when you know with certainty that a particular individual is dangerous and corrupt. It would be appropriate in this situation to warn those who are associating with him.

4. *When cooperating to give advice.* If you are cooperating with someone to correct the fault of a brother or sister, then it is permissible to speak about him or her in a limited capacity. Umar ibn Al-Khattab, may Allah be pleased with him, was once told that Abu Jandal drank alcohol while in Syria. Umar promptly wrote him a letter, which contained only, ⁅Ha Mim. The revelation of this Book is from Allah, Exalted in Power, Full of Knowledge,- Who forgives sin, accepts repentance, is strict in punishment, and has a long reach in all things. There is no god but He: to Him is the final goal.⁆[8] Abu Jandal immediately understood the message and repented.

In this situation, an individual approached Umar because he would be more effective in offering advice and influencing change in Abu Jandal. It would be acceptable to ask a righteous person, "My brother has a problem with such and such. Since you are good at correcting people gently, and he will respect your opinion, can

7 Agreed upon.
8 The Quran, 40:1-3.

you advise him?" This is allowed only if your intentions are pure. If your intention is to expose your brother and discuss his fault with someone else, then it is gossip.

5. *Calling someone by a commonly used nickname or label.* Referring to people by a label, such as "the one-eyed man" [9], is not backbiting only if they are commonly called this by others, with no tone of mockery, and the names do not bother them at all. However, it is of better character to select a more respectful way of referring to your brother or sister.

6. *Speaking of someone* who is flagrant in their sins. If you are talking about someone who brazenly sins and is not ashamed of his or her actions, then it is permissible to mention the sins of this person. Umar ibn Al-Khattab said, "The one who is unashamed has no sanctity." However, it is forbidden to speak of those sins that the person tries to hide from others, or those that he has already repented from.

What if I already talked about someone?
If you have fallen into backbiting, work on erasing the sins from your record. The following steps can be taken to seek Allah's pardon for what you have done.

1. *Repentance.*[10] Tawbah, or repentance, is the right of Allah upon the one who has sinned. In order to repent from backbiting, the Muslim must beg the forgiveness of Allah, immediately cease performing the sin, feel sincere regret, and resolve never to fall into the sin again.

2. *Seek the forgiveness from the injured party.* While repentance is the right of Allah, this second condition is the right of His servants.

---

9 In our society we might use a variation of these terms that may be offensive to some, such as "skinny", "heavyset", "gullible" etc.

10 Repenting to Allah, turning to Him, seeking His forgiveness, and sincerely regretting what has been done.

It is necessary to apologize and seek forgiveness from the one you wronged in order for the repentance to be complete. Without it, your repentance will be lacking and you will be held accountable for your deed on the Day of Judgment. If the wronged person knows that you gossiped and learned of what you said, then you must go to him and seek his pardon face to face.

If the individual is oblivious to your gossip, and would likely never find out, then it would be destructive to tell him. It would ruin relationships and create resentment in his heart. Instead, you should pray for him, seek forgiveness for both of you, and increase in your good deeds to make up for what he may take from you as a penalty on the Day of Judgment. The Prophetﷺ said,

> Whoever has wronged his brother in reputation or wealth should correct the situation immediately, before the Day of Judgment. For on that day, he will have no money and will pay with his good deeds instead. When all his good deeds have been taken, he will then carry the bad deeds of those he had wronged.[11]

The cure for Gheebah

Any sickness of the heart can be cured through knowledge and action.

1. *Knowledge.* If you have gossiped, you must know that this sin angers Allah. Imagine the good deeds that you worked so hard to earn transferred to someone else's scale, and someone else's bad deeds piled up on your scale. This thought should motivate you to change this harmful habit.

Realize that everyone has faults, including you. Instead of examining and talking bout others, be concerned with your shortcomings and direct attention to your self-improvement.

11 Agreed upon.

2. *Action.* The one who is committed to self-improvement should be keen on speaking only good words and avoid all speech that is motivated by doubtful intentions. You should be seeking reward with every word that your tongue utters. If what you intend to say is of no significance, the sunnah[12] is to keep silent. This will ensure that trivial and careless speech does not transform into speech.

Allah says in the Quran, ⟨Say to My servants that they should only say those things that are best.⟩[13] And the Prophetﷺ said, "Whoever safeguards his speech and his chastity, I can guarantee him Paradise."[14]

The Prophet once told Muadh ibn Jabal, "That is enough speech." Muadh asked, "Messenger of Allah, are we accountable even for what we talk about?" The Messenger answered, "Woe to you Muadh! Will people be thrown on their faces in the Hell-fire for anything more than what their tongues have sowed?"[15] Ibn Masud, may Allah be pleased with him, said, "Nothing is more in need of imprisonment than the idle tongue."

In order to rid yourself of the habit of backbiting, it is also important that you study the reasons that drive you to commit the sin. For example, if the foremost reason is that you are jealous of the one whom you backbite, then a remedy would be to make dua for the person. Pray that his or her blessings are increased and help the person in their affairs, in order to crush the feelings of envy.

If the motivation behind the gossip is anger and resentment, then seek refuge from shaitan and ask Allah to help you defeat your anger. By addressing the root cause, it is possible to prevent backbiting in the future and ensure that all of your words are pure and good.

---

12 The example set by Prophet Muhammad.
13 The Quran, 17:53.
14 Agreed upon.
15 Narrated by Tirmidhi.

Slander & Distasteful Language

Namimah is the Arabic word for slander and defamation with the intention of turning one person against another. It usually means to relate to someone what another person has said about him in order to stir up feelings of enmity. The individual who commits slander purposely sows resentment between Muslims.

Also in the realm of namimah is exposing anything that was intended to be private, whether in words, in writing, or by allusion. Whatever you glimpse from the private affairs of others, it is best to keep silent about it. When you witness or hear something that you know was intended to be secret, it is destructive to spread the news to others.

If you believe that some overwhelming good would come to people if they knew what you know, then it is excusable to disclose only what is necessary. For example, if you witnessed someone engaged in fraud, then it would be necessary to warn others and to testify against him in court if the oppression does not stop. However, if you know that an individual hoards wealth without giving in charity or commits indecencies in private, without impacting the affairs of anyone else, then spreading that information would be slanderous.

Allah says in regards to slander, {A defamer, going about with slander}[1] The Prophetﷺ said, "The person who persists in committing namimah will not enter Paradise."[2]

What Should I Do When I Hear Slander?

When you hear any form of slander described above, you must take the following steps.
1. *Discredit the Slander.* Refuse to believe what you were told. This is because the person who gave you the information is a slanderer, and his testimony is not accepted. Allah says in the Quran,

{ O you who believe! If a corrupt person comes to you with any news, ascertain the truth, lest you harm people without knowing, and afterwards become full of repentance for what you have done. }[3]

Even if the one who bears the news is a truthful person, you should still discredit what she has said. She is wrong because she attempted to create a rift between two Muslims. There is also the possibility that she was imprecise in telling you the news or that the person about whom she is speaking has already repented. It is also possible that the actions or words of the third person were not meant in a negative way, and were misunderstood by the speaker.

There are many possibilities and excuses that should come to our minds when we hear slander or gossip about our brother or sister—how can we judge someone based on mere hearsay? A man once entered upon Umar Ibn Abdul Aziz and told him what another had said behind his back. Umar immediately responded, "If you like, we can investigate what you have said. If it is untrue, then you are the one whom this verse refers to "If a wicked person comes to you with any news." If it is true, you are "A defamer, going about with slander." On the other hand, if you would prefer, we can forgive you." The

1 Al-Qalam, 11.
2 Agreed upon.
3 Al-Hujurat, 6.

man replied, "Forgiveness, Leader of the Believers! I will never do it again." However, if the intention of the speaker is only to warn sincerely, then the words are not considered slander.

2. *Identify the speech as slander.* If a person slanders, you should advise that person of the sin they are committing and its gravity.

3. *Detest the act of slander.* Reject the slander and refuse to take pleasure in listening to rumors and gossip. Slander is hated by Allah, and the Muslim should shun whatever displeases Him.

4. *Do not harbor any suspicion.* Make sure your heart is free of any suspicion toward your absent brother or sister who was slandered.[4]

5. *Dispel all doubt.* Do not be tempted to investigate or spy on your brother or sister.

6. *Do not relate the rumors to anyone.* Avoid mentioning the episode to others, so that you do not fall into slander yourself.

Offensive or Distasteful Language[5]

By offensive language, we mean words that are repulsive, rude, and discourteous. Such language includes cursing, profanity, and impolite expressions. The Messengerﷺ said, "The believer does not slander, curse, act shamelessly or obscenely."[6] Ibn Abbas, may Allah be pleased with him, said, "Verily Allah is discreet and noble. He pardons and He conceals. He refers [in the Quran] to intercourse only as 'touch'."

In line with these values, those who are of righteous character should avoid crude language and indecent speech. The young Islamic worker, as an example to others, should choose polite language over coarse expressions. Such politeness also includes avoiding speech about things that are forbidden, such as describing the opposite sex

4 Refer to article 2.
5 Al-Fahsh fi Al-Kalam.
6 Narrated by Tirmidhi.

or laughing about how people behave when they are drunk.

The Prophetﷺ said,

> Someone may say a word that seems insignificant to him,
> but it so pleases Allah that He will bestow upon this person
> His pleasure until the Day of Judgment. And someone may
> speak a word that he would never have imagined would
> mean so much, but it so incurs the anger of Allah that He
> will write His displeasure upon this person until the Day of
> Judgment.[7]

7 Narrated by Tirmidhi.

Useless Talk, Artificiality & Argumentation

Useless Talk

A young Muslim will be questioned by Allah regarding the use of her time. Every action brings us one step closer to death. Eminent death. It is unavoidable and every minute is closer than the last. When you have truly internalized this notion, you will be keen to use every second for Allah. The young Islamic worker knows that her time is a grant from Allah, through which she can draw closer to His pleasure.

When you understand the significance of time, it should have a marked effect on your speech. Idle chatter and pointless talk will take you nowhere. Even if the words are not sinful, they deter you from the remembrance of Allah and take up precious minutes that could be used more resourcefully. Allah tells us in the Quran, ﴾Successful indeed are the believers. Who are humble in their prayers, and who avoid vain talk.﴿[1] The Prophetﷺ said, "A sign of excellence in religion is to leave what does not concern you."[2]

---

1 The Quran, 23:1-3.
2 Narrated by Tirmidhi.

Life is nothing but time. When it is finished, you will be dead. We should not allow life to slip by while we are indulging in pointless activities and lost in our daily routines. The Prophetﷺ warned us to be wary of this heedlessness. Useless talk is a symptom of disregard for the blessing of time. Heﷺ said,

> A person will not take one step on the Day of Judgment before he is asked about four things: His time, how did he spend it? His youth, how did he take advantage of it? His money, from where did he earn it and how did he spend it? And his knowledge, how did he put it to use?[3]

The Messengerﷺ also said, "There are two blessings that most people are oblivious of: health and spare time."[4] Many people trade their health and time for things which will be of little use, whether in this life or the Hereafter.

As a busy Islamic activist or student trying to use your time to its maximum benefit, you might find it challenging to organize your time and take account of all that you say. It might seem sometimes that there are more obligations than you have time for and more distractions than you can be mindful of. However, if your intention is pure, you will be helped in achieving your goals. Here are some realistic tips that might help you optimize your time.

The Prophetﷺ used to supplicate, "Oh Allah, make the early morning blessed for my ummah." There is a special synergy to the early hours of the day, and the Muslim who uses it to her advantage will find increased productivity and a renewed impetus to use her time for Allah. This will help the young Islamic worker to avoid wasteful habits and vain talk throughout the day.

---

3 Narrated by Tirmidhi.
4 Narrated by Bukhari.

Learning from the experiences of earlier generations and reflecting upon the significance of time are other techniques to encourage judicious use of time. Do you remember what happened to those who used their time in vain speech and pointless pursuits? Where are they now? What have they achieved? Observe and contemplate the achievements and failures of people throughout history, with the intention of improving yourself. Allah says, ⟨Do they not travel through the land, so that their hearts may thus learn wisdom and their ears may thus learn to hear?⟩[5]

The knowledge that will help you defeat this habit is contemplation of the fleetingness of life. Know that death will strike at any moment. You will be held to account for every second you lived and every word you uttered. Allah says, ⟨Not a word does he utter but there is a sentinel by him, ready to record it.⟩[6]

Coupled with knowledge, there must also be parallel action and effort. Practice silence and speak when there is something good to say. If you struggle and work hard at this aspect of self development, Allah will grant you success and make it an easier task for you. He says in the Quran, ⟨Allah does not change the condition of a people until they change what is in their hearts.⟩[7]

Artificiality & Argumentation
The one who falls into this fault of speech is pretentious, artificial, and pedantic, using overly elaborate words, trying to impress others with his unrivaled eloquence. He occupies himself with argumentation, seeking out aggressive disputes, and frequently disagreeing with people, intending to prove them wrong and expose their ignorance.

5 The Quran, 22:46.
6 The Quran, 50:18.
7 The Quran, 13:11.

Do not mistake this fault of character with the art of choosing the best language in order to make the message of Islam appealing and understandable to people. That is a necessary duty which has its own reward. It does not fall under this category of speech. Artificialness in speech and argumentation are forbidden in Islam. Allah says, ❨Say: 'No reward do I ask of you, nor am I a pretender.'❩[8] The Prophetﷺ said,

> Those who are most loathsome to me and are distant from my gatherings are the people who chatter endlessly and who are pretentious and artificial in their speech.

The Messenger also said, "A sign that people have gone astray, after they had once been guided by Allah, is argumentation."[9]

The cure for this fault is rooted in knowledge and action. Learn about these vices, how they affect you and what causes them, and know that they bring about the anger of Allah. Knowledge will lead to action. Work to prevent the diseases that cause these symptoms, such as riya'[10] and arrogance.

It may be pride that motivates you to speak pretentiously and debase others. This pride and arrogance can be cured by seeking out the good actions that seem degrading or beneath you in the eyes of people. Such actions might be carrying someone else's load, doing behind-the-scene work, or cleaning the bathrooms in the mosque. Identify the actions that will stamp out any feelings of superiority and the need to impress, and perform them with enthusiasm and a sincere desire to please Allah.

Another method to combat affected speech and argumentation is to practice keeping silent. Make an extra effort to restrain your

8 The Quran, 38:86.
9 Tirmidhi.
10 See chapter one.

tongue from speech, except when keeping silent about something would be sinful, such as refraining from giving good advice or not forbidding evil. In those latter cases, speaking up is necessary and will be rewarded.

The young Islamic worker should strive to be someone who speaks with wisdom, confidence, and humility. She is one who invites others and calls them to Allah. She is setting an example in her mannerisms, the words she speaks and the conversations in which she engages. Dr. Sayyid Muhammad Nuh, in his book *The Journey's Pitfalls*,[11] gives a few more practical suggestions to Islamic workers on how to combat the bad habits of affected speech and argumentation. He gives valuable advice, which is summarized below.

Cultivate in yourself a deference and respect for others, even when they may have a different way of thinking. When Utbah ibn Rabi'ah came to tempt the Messengerﷺ to abandon his mission, implying that he could be dissuaded by money or power, the Prophet addressed him with utmost courtesy. The Prophet's ability to be courteous and civil to his enemy, while at the same time delivering his message with the utmost firmness and confidence, is indicative of his great character.

Avoid settings in which argumentation becomes a contest of wills and an end in itself. Although it is necessary for Muslims in American society to learn the art of speaking and polemics, it should not become a goal in itself or ego-oriented and should be rooted in a firm understanding of Islamic character and spirit.

Emulate the manners of the righteous people who speak with both confidence and humility. When you listen to the speech of a righteous servant, you will find a startling beauty and measure to their words. They shun argumentation for its own sake and seek to impress

---

11 Aafaat Ala At-Tareeq.

no one with their words. When someone disagrees with them, they assume the attitude of being convinced in their opinion but open to the possibility of being wrong. They speak only to please Allah. Only good comes from their lips.

Remember that speech is an action, not just an expression or a mere accessory to deeds. It is something that will weigh very heavily on your scale, for good or for bad. The young Muslim who remembers this will take effective steps to purifying his or her speech for the sake of Allah.

Lying & Breaking Promises

Lying

Lying is a sinful, treacherous habit. The young Muslim worker who suspects that he suffers from this habit should do everything he can to escape from its hold. It is possible to suffer from cowardice or greed and still be a Muslim, but it is impossible for a Muslim to be a liar. The Prophetﷺ said,

> Truthfulness leads to piety, and piety leads to Paradise. A man will keep telling the truth until it will be written in heaven that he is a 'truthful one.' Lying leads to shamelessness, and shamelessness leads to Hell. A man will keep telling lies, until one day it will be written that he is a 'liar.'"[1]

Heﷺ also said, "There are three characteristics that mark the hypocrite, regardless of whether he prays, fasts and calls himself a Muslim. They are: when he speaks, he lies; when he promises, he breaks his promise; and when he is entrusted, he betrays."[2]

The Prophet of Allah was once asked, "Is it conceivable for a Muslim to be a coward?"

1 Agreed upon.
2 Agreed upon.

"Yes," He answered.

"Is it conceivable for a Muslim to be greedy?" asked the questioner again.

"Yes."

"Is it conceivable for a Muslim to be a liar?"

"No," answered the Prophet⠹.[3]

As the Prophet so firmly stated, it is unacceptable for a Muslim to be a liar, because lying is one of the most hated sins in Islam. Lying is not befitting of a Muslim because in the end the liar is committed to sinning. One lie leads to many others, as the liar is forced to cover up her lie and hide her evil habit from the eyes of people. She will continue to hide and cover up lie after lie until she is discovered or until she stands on the Day of Judgment before The One who knows all that is hidden.

There are very few situations in which lying is permissible. Um Kulthum said, "I never heard the Prophet excuse any kind of lying, except three. A man who speaks to bring two people together after there was resentment between them, a man who speaks when he is in a war, and a husband and wife speaking to one another [in order to reconcile]."[4] In this latter situation, lying is allowed only when it will save a marriage from being damaged. When this is not the case, then lying is forbidden as in any other case.

Based on these three situations, there are similar circumstances in which a lie would be excusable. If a person asks a Muslim where his money is kept so that he can steal it, it would be acceptable for you to lie to protect your livelihood. If you are asked about a grave transgression that you committed that is known only by you and Allah, and no one else was affected by it, then it is permissible to lie. This is because Allah covers up the sins of His servants—pub-

3 Narrated by Malik.
4 Narrated by Muslim.

licizing transgressions is a transgression in itself. Finally, if you are asked about a secret that you share with a brother, and exposing that secret would damage his reputation, then it is permissible to deny the rumor about your brother.

There is a manner of speaking through which someone can avoid revealing anything embarrassing or sensitive, without revealing the truth. Umar ibn Al-Khattab said, "Isn't there enough in allusion and ambiguity to make lying unnecessary?" Intentional ambiguity is allowed only when there is a real need for it. However, when there is no pressing need, it is disliked. When one of the righteous people was sought after by someone he wished to avoid, he told his servant, "Tell the visitor, 'Look for him in the mosque.' But do not say I am not here, for that would be a lie."

Exaggeration is another habit to avoid, for it can lead to lying. It has become very common today to use exaggeration to emphasize a point. You might say, "I called you a hundred times and you didn't answer." Although you did not necessarily call your friend one hundred times, you are using the term to illustrate that you called many times. This is allowed only if you really did call many, many times, instead of just once or twice. In other words, exaggeration when in the form of a common expression or idiom is allowed, but it should be avoided in most contexts.

It is also a habit of ours to say that we do not want something that is offered, out of politeness, although we really desire it. When we are running late, we might say there was traffic—and there really was! But we know that it was really our procrastination or disorganization that made us late. It is best to steer clear of these gray areas and "white lies" that may make us insensitive to the sin of lying.

Do not lie carelessly. Ali ibn Abi Talib said, "The greatest mistake in front of Allah on the Day of Judgment is lying. It will bring the greatest regret of all regrets." Do not underestimate the habit and find excuses to engage in it, for this is one of the traps of the shaitan.

Breaking Promises

Fulfilling promises is an obligation in Islam, which means that you will be rewarded for doing it and punished for violating it. Guard your promises conscientiously, not letting even one slip by unfulfilled. Sometimes, we are so busy that we throw promises left and right, forgetting them and leaving them unattended. The promise of a Muslim should be dependable—his word is a rock-hard guarantee. Allah says in the Quran, ❴O you who believe! Fulfill all obligations.❵[5] Someone who makes a promise, secretly knowing that he will not fulfill it, has a symptom of hypocrisy. The Prophetﷺ said,

> Four characteristics—whoever has them all is a hypocrite. Whoever has some of them has a portion of hypocrisy inside him, until he abandons the characteristic. The four are: if he speaks, he lies; if he promises, he breaks his promise; if he gives an oath, he betrays; and if he quarrels, he is abusive.[6]

If you are confronted by some unforeseen obstacle that prevents you from fulfilling a promise, then breaking it would not be considered a sign of hypocrisy.

Keeping promises is a much broader principle than we might imagine. It goes beyond just sticking to the verbal confines of a promise to another. Keeping promises is part of loyalty, which is an essential aspect of the Muslim's character. Loyalty in a Muslim's life includes a staunch devotion to faith and its requirements. The feeling that Islam is itself a promise overwhelms the life of the young Muslim. She knows that this loyalty entails observing all of the commands of Allah, defending Islam, and holding allegiance to Islam

5 The Quran, 5:1.
6 Agreed upon.

above all else. Allah says, ⟨And fulfill your covenant with Me as I fulfill My Covenant with you.⟩[7]

Loyalty includes adhering to all contracts and treaties, whether with Muslims or non-Muslims. As long as the treaty does not violate the law of Allah, or force the Muslims to do something forbidden in Islam, they are obligated to respect the agreement. The Prophetﷺ said, "The Muslims stand by their agreements."[8]

Fulfilling vows to Allah is also included in the Islamic characteristic of loyalty. Allah says in the Quran, ⟨Allah will not call you to account for what is unpremeditated in your vows, but He will call you to account for your deliberate vows.⟩ An example of a vow in Islam would be to say, "If only Allah lets me get into this university, I will give half of my savings in charity." If the person then got into a university of his choice, he would be bound by his vow, and would have to give half of his savings in charity.

If the vow entails committing something which is forbidden, then you are obligated to break it and pay the prescribed, legal atonement for breaking the oath. The Prophetﷺ said, "Whoever makes a vow, and finds that he did not make the best choice in the vow, then he should make the prescribed atonement for his vow, and do what is better."[9] In general, it is best to avoid making vows when possible, especially when you are not fully informed of their consequences. Instead, do what is good without discrimination and without setting conditions between you and your Lord.

Loyalty also includes fulfilling debt. The Prophetﷺ said,

> Debts will be claimed on the Day of Judgment, except for those who fell into debt under three circumstances. The

---

7 The Quran, 2:40.
8 Narrated by Bukhari.
9 Narrated by Muslim.

one who became weak working for the sake of Allah and fell into debt in order to strengthen himself against the enemy of Allah, the one who died in the home of a Muslim and did not have the means to buy himself a burial shroud, and the one who feared that he would displease Allah and so fell into debt in order to get married. Allah will repay the debt on behalf of these people on the Day of Judgment.[10]

In his book *The Journey's Pitfalls*, Dr. As-Sayyid Muhammad Nuh gives some tips on how to strengthen your commitment and avoid negligence in your promises and Islamic work. A brief summary of some of those tips follows.

Remember that death will come suddenly, and that it is better to work hard and have strong will today. Rest, insha'allah, will come tomorrow in Paradise. Constantly ask Allah to give you the characteristics of honesty and loyalty, and to help you fulfill your covenants and promises. Take every promise you make with stern seriousness, and work hard to fulfill each one.

If you have trouble fulfilling promises because you are busy and disorganized, then watch your promise-making habits. Only make the promises that you know you can fulfill and work to keep them as if your life depended on it. Gradually incorporate an unwavering sense of responsibility, truth and loyalty in your life in order to actualize the beautiful, Islamic character that we are all aspiring for.

10 Narrated by Ahmad.

Other Faults of Speech

The faults of speech described in this section are betraying secrets, excessive joking and ridicule, praise, imprecision in speech, putting on a false front, withholding testimony and false witness, and listening to improper music or improper singing. These faults are forbidden because they breach the fundamental Islamic values of brotherhood, respect and love for the sake of Allah. It is essential that anyone working for the sake of Islam works to purify themselves, remove these faults, and replace them with the most beautiful speech.

The Prophetﷺ entrusted the believers with guidelines that preserve the brotherhood, love, and peace within their community. He warned each Muslim that the blood, wealth, and honor of his brother were not to be touched. He said in a hadith,

> The Muslim is the brother of every other Muslim. He does not betray him, reject him, nor turn against him. The honor, wealth, and blood of a Muslim must not be violated. Piety is here [the Prophet pointed to his heart]. The one who humiliates his brother in Islam has committed more than his share of evil.

Betraying Secrets

Disclosing someone's secret is a betrayal. It is disliked to disclose a secret even if there is reasonable compulsion, and forbidden when there is no pressing need for the secret to be disclosed. The Prophet said, "If someone speaks to you, looking over his shoulder [making sure that no one is listening], then consider what he has told you a trust."[1] He also said, "One of the worst people in front of Allah on the Day of Judgment is the one who had relations with his wife, then spread her secrets."[2]

If concealing a secret will result in some harm or calamity befalling an individual or society, then disclosing it becomes a necessity. It should not be said that this person is a troublemaker or trying to spread discord; he or she is concerned for the community and will be rewarded for that concern. The Messenger said,

> A private gathering is a trust, except for three: the gathering which will lead to wrongful bloodshed, the promiscuous gathering, and the gathering in which someone's property is unjustly confiscated.[3]

Excessive Joking & Ridicule

Excessive joking can be risky because it often borders on lying. When joking is based on a lie, it is forbidden. The Messenger said, "Woe to the one who tells lies in order to make people laugh. Woe to him. Woe to him."[4] When it is excessive, even if it does not involve lying, it is strongly discouraged. Too much laughter deadens the heart, creates malice and resentment, and can produce an atmosphere of disrespect.

1 Tirmidhi.
2 Muslim.
3 Ahmad.
4 Tirmidhi.

Joking is allowed when it is honest, good-spirited, and moderate. Such humor is relaxing, enjoyable, and fosters cheer and closeness between people. It is in fact a sunnah[5] of the Prophet. He used to joke from time to time in a decent, truthful manner. Once, an old woman came to the Prophet and asked him whether old people will be in Paradise. He joked with her, saying no. Later, when he saw her disappointment, he clarified that what he had said was true; no old people will be in Paradise because Allah will make all those who enter young again.

Ridicule, humiliating people, and exposing their weaknesses to laughter is another poor habit of speech. It can take the form of actions and words, through gestures, references, and imitation. Such mockery, which harms people's reputations, relationships, and feelings, is explicitly prohibited in the Quran,

> ⟨ *O you who believe! Let not some men among you laugh at others: It may be that the latter are better than those who laugh at them: Nor let some women laugh at others: It may be that those others are better than the ones who laugh at them.* ⟩ [6]

Praise

Praising someone in their presence is strongly disliked because it may damage the sincerity of the sister or brother being praised. Praise should similarly be avoided in someone's absence when there is a good chance the words will reach the one who was praised.

Praise is detestable because of its destructive effect on both the flatterer and the one being praised. Its impact is often devastating in relationships between people, and sometimes in the relationship with Allah. The individual who utters the praise may exaggerate or

5 The example of the Prophet which Muslims should strive to emulate.
6 The Quran, 49:11.

lie, leading to feelings of hypocrisy or duplicity in his own heart. He
may praise someone while harboring behind the words feelings of
resentment.

On the other hand, the one who receives praise may become
afflicted with pride and self-admiration, feeling smug about her
accomplishments and believing that she has achieved her peak po-
tential. Such feelings of self-satisfaction and overconfidence lead
to slackened effort and a decreased yearning for self-improvement.
Umar ibn Al-Khattab, may Allah be pleased with him, once said,
"Praise is slaughter."

A man once praised another in the presence of the Prophet𒑳.
Upon hearing the words of praise, the Prophet warned his companions of the dangers of praise.

"What disaster! You have killed your brother, should he hear what
you have said," said the Prophet. "If one of you feels compelled to
praise his brother and is convinced of the praise he is about to give,
he should say, 'I believe he is so, but only Allah knows the hearts and
Allah will be his Judge.'"[7]

There are some instances when praise can be given and remain
free of all of these dangers. In such cases, measured praise is allowed, and even recommended, if it encourages someone who needs
positive feedback, promotes good actions, and truly comes from the
heart. The Prophet𒑳 praised his companions on some occasions.
He𒑳 said once, "If there were to be a prophet after me, he would
have been Umar ibn Al-Khattab."[8] When the Prophet praised Umar
in this manner, he truly meant what he said and knew that his words
would not harm Umar's heart. Companions such as Umar were of
such high moral station that they would not succumb easily to self-
admiration and pride.

7 Agreed upon.
8 Tirmidhi.

Ali ibn Abi Talib, may Allah be pleased with him, used to say the following when someone praised him, "O Allah! Forgive me what they do not know, do not hold me responsible for what they have said, and make me better than what they say of me."

Imprecise Speech

Islam teaches us to speak with precision and certainty. In fact, such precision and exactness should pervade all matters in our lives. The Prophetﷺ encouraged exactness when he said, "No one should say, 'Whatever Allah wills, and whatever you desire,' but instead it should be said, 'Whatever Allah wills, and then whatever you desire.'"[9] Vague and careless speech can lead to errors or saying something that you did not mean. As in the hadith above, simply saying 'and' instead of 'then' makes it sound that the speaker is equating the will of Allah with the individual's will, even though such a meaning was not intended.

Putting on a False Front

This occurs when one says to others what they want to hear, even if it is false or unethical. Such a habit leads to duplicity—the person may praise people to their face and resent or berate them when they are absent. The Prophetﷺ said, "One of the worst slaves of Allah on the Day of Judgment is the two-faced person, who says one thing to one group and then another to a second group."[10] The one who is compelled to engage in deceit in order to avoid an impending harm is excused.

Aisha, may Allah be pleased with her, said, "Once, a man asked to meet with the Prophetﷺ. The Messenger, upon hearing that he wished to enter, said, 'Allow him to enter, for he is one of the worst

9 Abu Dawud.
10 Agreed upon.

of people.' When the Prophet met with him, his words with the man were restrained. When the man left, I asked him, 'O Messenger of Allah, you said such a thing about him, but you spoke to him courteously.' He answered, 'Aisha, the worst of people is the one whom you have no choice but to appease because you know he will abuse or insult you.'[11]

Withholding Evidence and False Testimony

Allah says in the Quran, ❴Conceal not evidence; for whoever conceals it, his heart is tainted with sin. And Allah Knows all that you do.❵[12] The companions of the Prophetﷺ relate the following incident:

> The Prophet asked us, "Shall I not tell you of the worst sins?" He asked this question thrice. We responded, "Yes." He continued, "Associating partners with Allah, dishonoring parents, and murder." After saying this, the Prophet, who had been leaning back, suddenly sat up. He said, "And lying and false testimony!" He repeated these last words again and again, until we wished that he would stop.[13]

Withholding evidence and false testimony are among the worst sins in Islam. The one who commits such evil is not just hiding the truth, but erasing it and promoting falsehood instead. It can incur great damage on all levels; it can destroy the personal lives of individuals and can harm the community on a grander scale. Speaking up in the face of wrongdoing is a religious obligation.

11 Agreed upon.
12 The Quran, 2:283.
13 Bukhari.

Singing and Music

Shaikh Sayyid Sabiq writes the following in his book, *Fiqh us-Sunnah:*

> Singing is merely speech. If the words are worthy, then the
> singing is good. If the words are improper, then the sing-
> ing is immoral. If the purpose of singing is beneficial, then
> it is allowed to sing and listen to songs. Such singing enliv-
> ens the heart and renews the Muslim's energy and resolve.
> Similarly, making use of the instruments that commonly
> accompany singing is also permissible.

Singing is worthwhile in a number of situations. A mother
who sings to her child, workers who sing during their la-
bor and toil, and people who sing during celebrations and
weddings are all utilizing this form of entertainment in a
positive way. Soldiers can sing and chant in order to invoke enthusiasm for jihad, as the companions did while
they were digging the trench in the Battle of the Trench.
All of these situations make use of the art in an acceptable
manner, provided that the words and references are pure
and good.

The proof for these statements is found in several *ahadith.*
Some of these texts follow:

Aisha, may Allah be pleased with her, narrated that Abu
Bakr once entered upon her and the Prophet. There
were two young girls who were singing and drumming
nearby, and the Messenger had covered himself with his
cloak. Abu Bakr scolded them, assuming that they were an-
noying the Prophet. The Prophet lifted the cloak from
his face and said, "Let them be, Abu Bakr. These are the
days of Eid."

The Prophetﷺ had recently returned from one of the battles. A young slave girl came to him upon his return and said, "O Messenger of Allah, I made an oath that I would sing and drum in front of you, if Allah were to return you safely to us." He replied, "If you have made an oath, then go ahead." So she played in his presence.

Many companions, including Abdullah Ibn Zubayr and Abdullah ibn Jafar, related that they used to listen to good, upright singing sometimes accompanied with instruments.

Songs that have immoral content are forbidden. One should stay away from music that arouses desire and sinful acts or weakens the goodness of the heart. The sayings of the Prophet that forbid music and singing refer to these harmful and immoral forms. Among these sayings is the following, "People of my *ummah* will drink alcohol, calling it by another name. They will play musical instruments and listen to female singers. Allah will cause the earth to swallow them, and He will make from among them monkeys and pigs."

This *hadith* does not necessarily mean that the people will physically turn into monkeys and pigs. Instead, it describes how the one who drowns in sin and desires becomes transformed through his behavior. His behavior resembles that of animals, and his conduct is unfit for a human being. [end of quotation from *Fiqh us-Sunnah*]

Physical Appetites

The young Muslim must learn to handle his or her physical appetites in a manner that is moral and permissible in Islam. An uncontrollable appetite for food and sex can lead the Muslim away from the pleasure of Allah.

Indulgence in Food and Drink

An indulgent appetite for food and drink can make a Muslim unhealthy and disinclined to worship and work for the sake of Islam. The Prophetﷺ said,

> The worst container to be filled to its utmost capacity is the stomach. It is enough for people to eat what will suffice for their energy, but if that is not attainable, then one third for food, one third for drink, and one third empty by which to breathe.[1]

Excessive and unhealthy eating is a destructive habit and if it consumes a person's life, it can lead him or her into a state of misery and self destruction. An indulgent appetite for food often leads to increased sexual drive and greed. Constantly enjoying an overfilled stomach also opens the door to too much sleep, obesity, a bad temper, and health problems.

1 Tirmidhi.

The solution to an unhealthy and uncontrollable appetite for food is to practice eating moderately. Moderate eating entails never eating unless you are hungry and never stuffing yourself. The Prophetﷺ said, "We are a people who do not eat until we are hungry, and when we eat, we do not fill ourselves."

The young Muslim should not fall into extremes by eating too little in order to avoid extravagance or to achieve a certain body form. It is not pious to starve yourself, obsessively diet, and deprive your body of necessary nutrition. Instead, it is ignorance of both your body's needs and the balanced principles of Islam. We were created to serve Allah, build civilization, and bring good to humanity. In order to achieve this, our bodies must be healthy, well-nourished, balanced, and strong.

Sexual Desire

A second physical appetite that can lead to sin is uncontrolled sexual desire. The Prophetﷺ said, "I have not left a more dangerous pitfall for men than the temptation of women."[2] Heﷺ also warned, "No man should be alone with a woman[3] unless she is accompanied by a mahram[4]."[5]

Sexual intercourse was created as a source of great benefit and satisfaction for human beings. One of those benefits is the creation of new generations and another is to allow physical satisfaction in a manner that is permissible in Islam. The marital relationship can invoke a joy that makes one look forward to the joys of the Hereafter and which renews the Muslim's longing for the reward of Allah.

However, if this drive is not handled correctly and not used in the context that Islam allows, it can lead to sinning. It can consume the

2 Agreed upon.
3 A woman who is not related to him.
4 A guardian: a male relative whom she cannot marry.
5 Agreed upon.

mind of a young person, leading to weakened self control, attachment to material life, and immorality and sin. Depending on the circumstances of the young Muslim, there is always a means by which this temptation can be relieved.

If the young Muslim is not married, he should know the dangers of allowing sexual desires to control his behavior. It can lead to the anger of Allah and weakened willpower. After realizing the severity of this situation, he should take action by lowering his gaze. Lowering the gaze is a weapon that the young Muslim can use to prevent these desires from overtaking him. The Prophetﷺ said, "The desirous look is a poisoned arrow of shaitan. Whoever leaves it fearing Allah, Allah will give him faith that he tastes as sweetness in his heart."[6]

One can also overcome her desires by constantly engaging herself in Islamic work. She can also develop worthy pastimes to keep herself busy and productive, such as sports or reading. Working to control sexual desires is an exercise in patience and willpower that will fortify the young Muslim for the rest of his or her life. Voluntary fasting will greatly strengthen this willpower, as will seeking the help of Allah through supplication.

Finally, the young Muslim who is struggling with this temptation may consider marriage if he is capable and ready to bear the responsibilities. The Messengerﷺ said, "Young people! If you are able to bear the responsibilities of marriage, then marry. It controls the gaze and guards the chastity. Whoever is still unable to marry should fast, for fasting will be a shield for him."[7] The young Muslim who is already married should work to control her gaze and strengthen her willpower. She should also occupy herself with what is good and beneficial so that her thoughts do not stray and wander to what is forbidden.

6 Al-Hakim.
7 Agreed upon.

Material Attachments:
Adoring Life, Self & Wealth

❴ Verily, you prefer the life of this world. But the Hereafter is better and more enduring. ❵ [1]

Adoring Life

Read and contemplate the following sayings of the Prophetﷺ. Realize how trivial this world is compared to the bewildering world of the Hereafter that awaits all of us.

> This world, compared to the Hereafter, is like dipping your finger in the sea. How much water is on your finger, compared to the sea? [2]

> If this world was worth a fly's wing in front of Allah, the disbeliever would have been denied even a drink of water. [3]

---

1 The Quran, 87:16-17.
2 Bukhari and Muslim.
3 Tirmidhi, Sahih.

This world is a prison for the believer, a paradise for the disbeliever.[4]

Whoever loves this world loses something of the Hereafter, and whoever loves the Hereafter loses something of this world. So opt for what is lasting over what will end.[5]

This world is sweet and lush, and Allah has established you therein to see what you will do. When the world was laid before the Children of Israel, they became lost in its jewels, women, perfumes, and adornment.[6]

It was also said, "The one who longs for this world is like one who drinks from the sea. The more he drinks, the more his thirst increases, until he dies of thirst."

This condemnation of worldly attachment applies to the one whose only concern is to satisfy his desires and fantasies. He will satisfy his desires regardless and accepts no boundaries or guidelines. Running after women, alcohol, and all forms of play and entertainment, he knows neither discipline nor decency. Imagine the state of humanity if everyone adopted such behavior—there would be no desire for truth, no establishment of justice, and no concern for others. We would be a community of losers, acting on every impulse and rotting in a stagnant, destroyed society.

If you find traces of adoration of life in yourself, the cure lies in two elements: knowledge and action. First, know that this world pales in comparison to the Hereafter. You will find no security or peace of mind in this world, so invest instead in the Hereafter. Know that you are only passing through this world and not settling here for good.

4 Muslim.
5 Al-Hakim, Sahih.
6 Tirmidhi.

You are like a traveler walking through and trying to sow as many good deeds as you can in order to reap them later in the Hereafter. Know that death is just around the corner and that it comes suddenly. Once it comes, there will be no second chance and no return.

Secondly, act! Some of the actions that you can take to release the world's hold on your heart and desires are described here. Begin to practice zuhd—worldly detachment coupled with moderation—in its true meaning. The true meaning of zuhd is to hold the world in the palm of your hand and not in your heart. You use the good that Allah gave you in His service, guiding, helping, and leading people to good. Do not allow adoration of this life to conquer your heart. Take from this world only what is needed to maintain your heart and soul and allows you to fulfill your responsibilities.

Allah says in the Quran, {And seek, with the wealth that Allah has bestowed on you, the Home of the Hereafter, but do not forget your portion in this world.}[7] Thus, the balanced young Muslim is not deeply attached to this life but he also does not abstain from its every pleasure, which will put him on the track to exhaustion and breakdown. The Prophetﷺ said, "The best of all matters is what is balanced."[8]

At the time of the Prophet, three men agreed amongst each other to go to the extreme in worship and denial of this life. One vowed to fast non-stop, another to spend every night in prayer, and the third to practice celibacy. The Prophetﷺ taught them a lesson, responding, "As for me, I both fast and break my fast. I pray for some of the night and sleep for the other, and I have relations with my wives. Whoever strays from my sunnah is not of me."[9]

7 The Quran, 28:77.
8 Al-Baihaqi.
9 Bukhari and Muslim.

Self-Adoration

◊ But selfishness has been made present in the souls of men... ◊ [10]

This verse reminds us that greed and attachment is present in the human soul, always tempting and urging. The selfishness of self-adoration sabotages our attempts to sacrifice and be generous. It prevents us from the giving, of wealth, time, effort, and advice. Our love toward ourselves and our material possessions are a test for us. Are we able to conquer this built-in, negative characteristic and rise to lofty heights in goodness and character? Or will self-adoration bring us down into the depths of disobedience and greed?

The cure for an overpowering love of the self involves a combination of knowledge and action. In terms of knowledge, you must convince yourself of the harm that this characteristic can inflict on your future in this world and the Hereafter. In this world, greed and strong attachment to the self can lead to oppression and selfishness. The Prophet said, "Beware of greed. It invited those who came before you and led them to spill each other's blood. It called to them, and led them to violate what was sacred. It called to them, and led them to break blood-relations." [11]

Take time out to learn about the great merits of selflessness, giving, and considering the needs of others. Allah praises those who are in service of others, sometimes at their own expense, *◊ They give them preference over themselves, even though poverty was their own lot. ◊* [12]

Ali ibn Abi Talib is an outstanding example of this type of altruism, offering his own soul in exchange for the wellbeing of the Messenger and his religion. Ali slept in the bed of the Prophet on

10 The Quran, 4:128.
11 Al-Hakim, Sahih.
12 The Quran, 59:9.

the eve of the migration to Madinah, knowing well that he risked death at the hands of those who intended to murder the Prophet. In the Battle of Yarmuk, Ikrimah ibn Abi Jahl, Suhail ibn Amr, and others were martyred. It is related that before they passed away, a water carrier found one of them wounded on the battlefield and offered him water, only to find the wounded soldier sending him to tend to another wounded brother. Each one said, "Give water to him first." Each one preferred his brother over himself and each one died before he could feel the cool water in his own throat.

Once, a companion received a goat's head as a generous and tasty gift. Upon receiving the meal, he immediately checked himself and thought, "My brother needs it more than me." So he sent it to his brother's house where it was passed on to another in need. And so the meal traveled from house to house, each person thinking of someone else who might be hungry or might enjoy the gift. The goat's head was passed through seven homes, until it ended up at the home of the first man.

Aishah, may Allah be pleased with her, related that once she sacrificed a goat and gave most of it to charity. The Prophetﷺ asked her, "What remains of the goat?" She said, "Nothing but the shoulder." The Prophetﷺ replied, "Everything but the shoulder."[13] The Prophet meant that just because most of the goat was given away did not mean there was little left; it remained plentiful as reward in front of Allah.

The actions that you can take to conquer selfishness are several. Gradually train yourself to give in different areas of your life and of different things that you love. Start small and build up to higher levels of generosity that may be more challenging for you. By starting gradually and consistently, you can ingrain generosity and selflessness in your character.

13 Tirmidhi.

Work to conquer the obstacles that prevent you from giving freely of your time, effort, and possessions. Indulging in habits that waste time and divert attention can make you insensitive and selfish. Feeling too secure in this temporal life can make you cling tightly to earthly possessions and mundane passions that do not matter. All this will vanish when death suddenly leaps upon you.

Adoring Wealth and Possessions

Money, in and of itself, is not evil. In fact, it may sometimes be a great advantage if it is used wisely. Money can be used to achieve good things in this life and is described in the Quran as a means of support and benefit. Allah says,

> ﴿ *To those incapable of responsibility do not give away your wealth, which Allah has made a means of support for you, but feed and clothe them therewith, and speak to them words of kindness and justice.* ﴾ [14]

The Prophet☺ said,

> There are only two kinds of people who may be envied—a man whom Allah has given wealth and who sacrifices it at his own expense for the truthful cause, and a man who is given knowledge that he acts upon and teaches to others. [15]

However, we all know that money can also sow mischief and greed in the heart of the one who possesses it. Money is harmful when it is strongly coveted by its owner or when it is gained through unlawful means. It is destructive when it is spent carelessly, becomes a means to boast and show off, and distracts time and attention from the worship

14 The Quran, 4:5.
15 Agreed upon.

of Allah. Money, when spent on trivial matters and enjoyments, can lead its owner to excessiveness, gluttony, and finally to deeds that are disliked by Allah. It has the power to gradually desensitize the soul to the ephemeral nature of this life. Allah says in the Quran, ﴾And know that your possessions and your children are but a trial.﴿[16]

The Prophetﷺ said, "There are three things that destroy: Greed, desire, and self-admiration."[17] He also said, "There are two characteristics which cannot both be present at the same time in a believer: Greed and bad manners."[18] In another hadith, the Prophetﷺ said, "O Allah! I seek refuge in You from greed, from cowardliness, and from senility in old age."[19]

Greed is a characteristic which conceivably may be present in the hearts of some Muslims. However, it has limits beyond which no Muslim should stray—beware if you feel yourself approaching these boundaries. The final limit to greed is withholding what another is rightfully entitled to. Such an entitlement may be a religious duty, such as zakah and supporting one's children and family. There are also obligations which emanate from a basic sense of decency and graciousness which should be typical of any Muslim. Such duties include giving gifts to relatives, friends, and brothers and showing hospitality towards guests, tending neither toward excessiveness nor stinginess.

The young Muslim who fulfills these obligations necessitated by her religion and good manners, without grudges, or favors expected in return, has liberated herself from the temptation of greed. She is also rewarded for fulfilling her religious and social responsibilities.

Wealth and favors should not be dispensed with the expectation of a favor in return, improved social status, or for the sake of friendship

16 The Quran, 8:28.
17 Tabarani: Hasan.
18 Tirmidhi.
19 Bukhari.

and popularity. Generosity is excellent when it comes from the goodness of the heart and is exercised without resentment or expecta-
tions. Such a surplus of generosity is commendable when the Muslim
hopes only to gain extra favor and reward from her Lord.

For one who is tested with a tendency toward selfishness and
greed, the cure lies in two elements: knowledge and action. The
young Muslim must educate herself of the harmful effects of greed
and the extent to which it is disliked by Allah. She should learn about
the beautiful reward for generosity and the dignity in the sight of
Allah of one who possesses such a characteristic. As for the one who
is plagued with greed and does not try to overcome it, her standing in
front of Allah and among people is one of humiliation and pettiness.
The Prophetﷺ said,

> The openhanded, generous person is near to Allah, near
> to the hearts of people, near to Paradise, and distant from
> Hell. The stingy, greedy person is far from Allah, far from
> the hearts of people, far from Paradise, and near to Hell.
> An ignorant, generous person is more beloved to Allah
> than a greedy person devout in worship.[20]

In order to rid yourself of greed and attachment to material things,
you should also study the purpose of wealth and why it was created by
Allah. Do not value wealth and material possessions more than they
deserve. Purify your intention in using money and spending it. Know
truly from your heart that spending money in a good cause does not
decrease your wealth, but instead multiplies it. Release the grip your
heart holds on wealth and give freely. Allah says, ❴And nothing do
you spend in the least in His cause but He replaces it: for He is the
Best of those who grant Sustenance.❵[21] The Prophetﷺ said,

20 Tirmidhi.
21 The Quran, 34:39.

Charity does not decrease wealth in the least. Pardoning another only increases you in nobleness in front of Allah. And when you humble yourself for the sake of Allah, Allah will elevate you.[22]

Having realized the merits of charity, the second step to overcome greed is action. Exercise moderation in your lifestyle. The Prophetﷺ said,

> Three characteristics will set you free: Being in awe [*taqwa*] of Allah whether in public or by oneself, caution in spending whether wealthy or poor, and dealing fairly whether pleased or angry.

Whoever accustoms herself to a moderate lifestyle will have no difficulty spending her extra money in a manner that is most pleasing to Allah.

Do not worry about provision. Anxiety over money will lead you to stockpile your wealth and resist giving it to good causes. When you convince yourself that Allah will provide for you as long as you have taken reasonable measures to secure yourself a living, you will have nothing to worry about. Allah says in the Quran, ﴿There is no moving creature on earth but its sustenance depends on Allah.﴾[23]

You must also convince yourself that true wealth is much more than just material possessions and money. Your health, happiness, contentment, tranquility, and relationships are also part of your wealth. Wealth can also be the many opportunities for doing good that are available to you through your money, your children, your time, your Islamic work, and your manners. The ability to love and be compassionate towards people is a form of wealth. Good intentions for every

22 Muslim.
23 The Quran, 11:6.

thing you do will transform all actions into good ones, multiplying your reward in the Hereafter. When you view all of these dimensions of wealth, and count it in addition to what sits in your bank account, material possessions will diminish in comparison.

When comparing yourself to others, look towards those who are less fortunate than you in material and social stature so that it is easier to feel thankful. When you acknowledge those who have less than you, it gives you confidence and contentment with whatever Allah provides for you. You appreciate what you have as a great blessing and favor. The Prophetﷺ said,

> Look to those who are beneath you, and do not look to those who are above you. Such is better for you that you do not belittle the blessings Allah has given you.[24]

However, when you compare yourself to others in piety and religious devotion, aspire to those who are above you. Compare yourself with the companions and those who have given their lives in the service of Allah, not to discourage but to motivate. Such perspective will give you the ambition and perseverance to reach higher stations in the Hereafter, which belong to those who work and sacrifice for the sake of Allah.

24 Agreed upon.

Anger

Anger can be constructive or destructive. It is important to know when anger can be appropriate and useful and when it is sinful. Constructive anger is that which is exercised in the defense of good or in the face of oppression. This anger may appear when the sacred is taken lightly or when the laws of Allah are ignored.

Anger, as we commonly know it, is more often damaging than favorable. Tempers may flare because of pride, greed, ridicule, or argumentation. Just as the contexts of anger are many, so are its degrees. People differ in their ability to master and control their anger, and the strength of the emotion varies greatly from person to person. As always, the ideal Muslim is one who is moderate in the expression of his anger.

Excessive, uncontrollable anger is wrong and damaging. It drives a person to lose control over his will and mind, acting without foresight or reason. Often, it may lead to sin and irreparable harm. A complete lack of anger is similarly undesirable, as the person responds to unjust situations by retreating and giving in. Such a person may lose his sense of honor and confidence.

The ideal that we are aiming for is an anger that is of wise purpose, moderate expression, and appropriate circumstance. Such a young Muslim is in complete control of his emotions and only releases them if he deems it will bring about benefit and good. When anger is inappropriate or useless, he controls it and hides it. Abu Said Al-Khudri relates that the Prophet☘ said,

> People were created of different temperaments. Some are slow to anger, quick to pardon. Some are quick to anger, quick to pardon. And yet others are quick to anger, slow to pardon. The best of them are those that are slow to anger, quick to pardon, and the worst of them are the quick to anger, slow to pardon.

What is Permissible in the Moment of Anger

When someone wrongs you by committing a sin, it is inappropriate to respond with a similar offense. If someone backbites or slanders you, it is wrong to do the same in revenge. If someone insults you, it is wrong to reply with rudeness. Instead, leave it to those who are in positions of power to take care of the matter. You may also try to forgive the person, in hope of a great reward in the Hereafter. The Prophet☘ said, "If someone abuses you, do not do the same wrong to him."[1]

Although it is wrong to respond to an insult with a similar one, you are allowed to defend yourself by speaking only what is true, permissible, and appropriate. For example, you may respond to an insult by saying calmly, "That is because you don't understand." This would be truthful because whenever anyone commits a sin, there is an element of ignorance in him or her. You could also say something completely truthful such as, "Who are you to think that? You are only a mere person!" Such a response may help to quell your own anger and give you the satisfaction of defending yourself in an upright manner without engaging in anything that is wrong or untruthful.

1 Ahmad.

Once, when two companions were arguing with each other, one told the other, "Are you anything but a person from the tribe of Hadheel?"

"And do you think you are anything but a person from the tribe of Umayyah?" the second retorted. Thus, although they argued angrily, these two companions refrained from deep personal insult and uncontrollable anger.

The Prophetﷺ said, "Upon insult, the one who began is at fault, unless the second exceeded the permissible."[2] The Prophet allowed the one who is insulted room for defending oneself, by responding in a manner that is truthful and decent. However, it is best to forgive. When you are angry, it is too easy to slip beyond what is allowed and stray into what is forbidden. Often, when people are angry, they lose control and cannot abide by these conditions. That is why it is recommended to pardon the affront, especially if you know you have an issue with controlling anger.

Dealing with Anger

First, know the harm that comes from anger: there are numerous sayings of the Prophet on the pitfalls of anger. Uncontrolled anger is from shaitan and deprives a young Muslim of her self-control and common sense. It is a means through which ill feelings can penetrate the best of relationships; a moment's anger can estrange a husband and wife from each other, divide good neighbors, and drive communities to war.

A man once asked the Prophetﷺ to give him a simple and straightforward command to act upon. The Prophet answered, "Do not get angry." The man asked for another counsel, and the Prophet said again, "Do not get angry."[3] The Prophet said on another occasion,

2 Muslim.
3 Bukhari.

Strength is not in bodily might. Rather, strength lies in he who is able to control himself in the moment of anger.[4]

Know the merits of controlling your anger. Allah says in the Quran,

> ❴ *Be quick in the race for forgiveness from your Lord, and for a Garden whose width is that of the heavens and of the earth, prepared for the righteous. Those who spend, whether in prosperity, or in adversity; who restrain anger, and pardon others—for Allah loves those who do good.* ❵ [5]

The Prophet said, "The one who restrains his anger, although he is capable of acting on it, will be summoned by Allah in front of all creation to choose which of the women of Paradise he wishes."[6]

The Prophet also said to a man named Ashaj Abd Al-Qays, "You have two qualities that are beloved to Allah: forbearance and patience."[7] The forbearance that the Messenger describes in this statement is disinclination to anger, which comes from a high degree of self-control and a love for doing what is true and right. Achieving this high level comes from constant practice.

Al-Hasan detailed several prominent characteristics of a Muslim. He highlighted them in a beautiful character sketch,

> Of the characteristics of a Muslim: steadfastness in religion, resolve during ease, faith with certainty, knowledge with forbearance, gentleness with intelligence, generosity in what is rightful, prudence in wealth, excellence in prosperity, and patience in difficulty. He is not controlled by anger or desire and forgives the one who is ignorant and the one who wrongs him.

---

4 Bukhari.
5 The Quran, 3:133-134.

6 Tirmidhi: hasan.
7 Muslim.

Finally, know that Allah is capable of acting on His anger towards His servants. However, He, in His grace and mercy, chooses to pardon them and give them more chances.

The actions you can take to conquer anger are several. Avoid circumstances in which you normally become angry. Work on the characteristics in yourself that lead you to anger easily. If pride is the underlying cause of your short temper, then strive towards humility. If you become angry over finances and money, then try to set your priorities straight and observe caution in your spending. If you tend to become angry during debates, then keep quiet during discussions until you have learned to control your feelings. Address the faults in your character that lead you to anger before your temper is given a chance to flare up. Say, "I seek refuge in Allah from the cursed shaitan," when you feel anger rising in your heart. The Prophetﷺ advised Muslims to say this during moments of anger.

If anger does not dissipate, change your body's position. If you were standing, take a seat and calm yourself. If you were seated, lie down. Calming your mind and body will help the anger to cool. Working yourself into a frenzy will only heat up your body, stir your emotions, and make the anger impossible to control. Abu Hurayrah said, "When the Prophetﷺ got angry, he would sit if he had been standing. If he got angry while sitting, he would lie down. In such a manner he would calm his anger."[8]

If you still cannot quell your anger with all of these measures, make wudu. The coolness of the water and the process of performing an act of worship for Allah will help you calm down. The Prophet said,

> Anger is from shaitan, and shaitan was created from fire. Fire is extinguished with water. So if you become angry, make wudu.[9]

8 Ibn Abi-Dunya.
9 Abu Dawud.

Resentment & Envy

Resentment

When a person suppresses his anger, allowing it to build without addressing it, anger will change to resentment. Resentment is the result of suppressed anger that has deeply embedded itself in a person's thoughts and feelings. This product of anger is often long-term and extremely destructive. Resentment leads to other faults of character, including envy, backbiting, spreading secrets, aggressive behavior, and indifference.

The young Muslim activist who discovers the signs of resentment in her heart can work to remove it through two venues: knowledge and action. She must know the harm of resentment towards her sisters and realize that it inflicts the most pain on her own self, before any one else. A resentful heart is plagued with thoughts and images, to the point of obsession, and such a heart can only think of finding ways to get back at another. If this resentment is not resolved, such a Muslim faces the possibility of punishment from Allah if she does not repent beforehand.

It is not enough to know the dangers of resentment—act upon that knowledge. Whatever feelings of resentment urge you to do or think, strive for the opposite. If resentment drives you to wish that some inconvenience or harm would befall someone, make dua that such a person is blessed with ease in his matters. If you are tempted to backbite, spread a rumor, or divulge a secret, hold your tongue and occupy it with something better. If you feel like ignoring someone and being cold towards them, instead strive to be sincere and warm when you greet them.

Perform the small, everyday actions that will bring your heart closer to that person, such as visiting them when they are sick, calling them on the phone, or giving them a gift. Make sure such an action is done with sincerity, hoping only for the pleasure of Allah.

Abu Bakr, may Allah be pleased with him, once swore never to give any financial support to one of his relatives who depended on him, because that person had been one of the instigators of the rumors slandering Aishah, his own daughter and the wife of the Prophet. But Allah revealed the following verse,

> {*Let not those among you who are endued with grace and abundance swear against helping their kinsmen, those in want, and those who have left their homes in Allah's cause: let them forgive and overlook, do you not wish that Allah should forgive you?*} [1]

Upon hearing this reminder, Abu Bakr immediately said, "Yes, I wish that [for Allah to forgive me]." Despite being deeply wronged, Abu Bakr resumed giving aid to his relative and fought off the ill feelings and resentment he experienced.

1 The Quran, 24:22.

Envy

Envy is to wish that someone's good blessings would be taken away from her or that harm would befall her. Although it is only an action of the heart, and sometimes has few outward signs, it can be the source of deep-seated animosity and sin. In extreme cases, envy can actually drive someone to act upon the ill feelings by harming someone and causing their downfall from a situation of blessing and happiness. An envious person piles sins upon sin and will be punished accordingly if she does not repent.

Allah says in the Quran, ⟨Many of the followers of the Book wish that they could turn you back into unbelievers after your faith, out of envy from themselves, even after the truth has become manifest to them.⟩[2] Prophet Muhammadﷺ said, "Do not envy one another, abandon one another, hate, nor shun one another. Be, O slaves of Allah, brothers."[3]

Envy eats away at your sanity and happiness and can penetrate all of your thoughts. Indeed, envy destroyed nations before us and religions before us—it is conceivable that it may destroy us too, whether as individuals or communities. We were directed to seek refuge from envy. In Surah Al-Falaq, Allah says,

⟨ *Say: I seek refuge in the Lord of the dawn. From the mischief of created things; from the mischief of darkness as it overspreads; from the evil of those who practice secret arts; and from the evil of the envious one as he envies.* ⟩[4]

If the envier hates what he is doing to himself and to others, despises the envy that he finds in his heart, and strives to prevent it from having any effect on his outward behavior, he has succeeded in avoid-

---

2 The Quran, 2:109.
3 Agreed upon.
4 The Quran, 113:1-5.

ing envy's harm. If a passing thought stirs up feelings of envy, he is
not to blame. Occasional negative thoughts are natural to the human
mind. As long as they do not dwell long enough in the heart to lead
to action, they are not sinful thoughts.

Jealousy is different from envy. To be jealous of someone is to wish
that you had something that he or she has, without wishing that such
a blessing be removed from the other. Competitiveness is also different. It is to wish to be like or surpass your peers without wishing to see
them humiliated or put down. Jealousy and competition are allowed
if they are in good matters related to this world. They are actually
encouraged in matters related to the Hereafter and to the pleasure
of Allah. Allah says in the Quran, ❨The seal thereof in Paradise will
be Musk—And for this let those who have aspirations compete!❩[5]
The Prophetﷺ said,

> Jealousy is only appropriate in two instances: to be jealous
> of a man who was given wealth and spent it all for the sake
> of the truth, and of a man who was given knowledge, acted
> upon it, and taught it to others.[6]

The previous verse and hadith illustrate that competition in superior deeds, such as spending for the sake of Allah and gaining knowledge, is commendable. This mutual encouragement brings about
purification in this life, reward in the Hereafter, and disregard for
the paltry pursuits of material life.

Indignation over an outright wrongdoing is not envy, but is obligatory on every Muslim. The Muslim who acts upon it will be rewarded, and the one who does not will be punished. For example,
a Muslim should disapprove of a politician who rose to power via
bribery, and this should not be interpreted as envy of status and

5 The Quran, 83:26.
6 Agreed upon.

position. Instead, it is concern over the welfare of society and the morals of the community.

The Causes of Envy

Envy arises when many people rush to get a share of a particular aspect of life, such as money, status, popularity, or education. When some people succeed in these areas, others envy them. This will always happen when the hearts of people are keen on attaining the benefits of this temporal world, instead of being focused on the Hereafter. Those who remain steadfast in their service to Allah do not envy. They desire the pleasure and reward of Allah. For that, the sky is the limit no matter how many people pursue it.

Envy can be caused by a naturally selfish, jealous disposition, which resents any good that is bestowed on the servants of Allah. Such a person winces when she thinks of the good that another person has and is secretly content that another goes through difficulty. Her jealousy might lead her to feel that the good things granted by Allah to other people are at her own expense—or out of her own pocket! Such envy may be the result of a natural disposition that she is tested with, and its cure is found in persistence and patience. The solution to envy lies in the combination of knowledge and action.

You must know the dangers of envy in this life and the Hereafter. In the Hereafter, you will reap the sins of envy, and in this life, you will live in pain and anxiety, fretting over the blessings given to others. All of the resentment and mental agony will not increase you in blessings, abilities, or talents—in the end, you will only get what Allah has written for you. Moreover, your envy will not prevent another person from increasing in good, for that person will also get whatever was intended for him. Know also the reward of striving to improve your character. Even if you feel a natural inclination to envy and jealousy, the harder you work to rid yourself of the vice, the greater your jihad and the greater your reward.

In addition to gaining knowledge, here are some actions you may take to address the vice of envy. Investigate the underlying causes of your envy, whether resentment, anger, or attachment to this life, and work to purge it from your character. The most common cause of envy is craving the artificial symbols of prosperity in this world: status, popularity, wealth, beauty, and power. You must work to reframe your understanding of this world, so that those temptations no longer drive you to destruction.

Perform the opposite of whatever your envy urges you towards in order to defeat it. Be patient in striving to change yourself. It will not come easily, but eventually Allah will give you success and envy will no longer be an intrinsic aspect of your character. Thus, make dua for those whom you envy, help them, and humble yourself when you are around them. Speak only good of them, visit them, call them, and present them with gifts. Such actions, even if they are difficult at first, will eventually become easy for you and will help remove envy out of your thoughts.

Vanity & Self-Deception

Vanity

Vanity is to be proud of your talents or personal characteristics, whether hereditary, physical, financial, or knowledge-based. This pride is paired with the inner feeling that these gifts came about through your own brilliance and hard work. The one possessing this mindset takes the blessings of Allah for granted. He forgets that it was Allah who bestowed upon him those abilities and talents in the first place.

Vanity is a disease of the heart that is independent of social context. Even if a man were the last alive on earth, he still may feel proud and self-sufficient. If vanity leads a Muslim to disdain and belittle others, even if in his thoughts, he has become arrogant. If it leads one to believe that she always has the favors of Allah, is saved, and doesn't need to improve herself, then she has been fooled by a false sense of security. If vanity leads a Muslim to follow her own opinions and desires, confident that her views and opinions are better than others, then she is deceiving herself.

On the other hand, rejoicing in the talents, abilities, and qualities that Allah gave you and using them in the service of Allah is not vanity. Instead, this is confidence and self-assuredness that is based on gratefulness and trust in Allah, a necessary quality in a young Islamic worker's character.

Vanity can affect even the best of people. Allah says, chastising the vanity in the hearts of some of the Muslims during the Battle of Hunayn, ❴Assuredly Allah did help you in many battlefields and on the day of Hunayn: Behold! Your great numbers pleased you, but they availed you nothing—the land, for all that it is wide, did constrain you, and you turned back in retreat.❵[1] Allah also says in the Quran,

> ❴ *Those who avoid great sins and shameful deeds, only falling into small faults, verily your Lord is ample in forgiveness. He knows you well when He brings you out of the earth, and when you are hidden in your mothers' wombs. Therefore do not attribute purity to your souls: He knows best who it is that guards against evil.* ❵[2]

Also, ❴And show not favor, seeking worldly gain!❵[3] meaning do not admire the quantity of your good deeds, feeling secure and entitled to the mercy of Allah, only to find yourself one day destroyed. The Prophetﷺ said, "There are three things that destroy—greed, desire, and self-admiration."[4]

Ibn Masud, may Allah be pleased with him, said, "Destruction lies in two things—despair and vanity." Despair and vanity are devastating because happiness in this life and the Hereafter only comes about through genuine effort, willpower, and racing to good. The one who despairs exerts no effort and has no willpower. The vain person believes that she has already made it and thus does not feel the humility and eagerness that will help her race to improve herself.

How can we go about curing this fault, vanity? Learn about the dangers of vanity. Read, listen, and study this disease of the heart until you are fully convinced that it is a destructive quality that must

1 The Quran, 9:25.
2 The Quran, 53:32.
3 The Quran, 74:6.
4 Tabarani.

be dispelled. Know and internalize the belief that all talents, personal qualities, and abilities are from Allah and that He is fully capable of taking them away.

In Surah Al-Kahf, Allah tells us the story of a man who owned lush, thriving gardens and believed that they came of his own resourcefulness. Then one day, he realized too late the foolishness of vanity,

> *So his fruits and enjoyment were encompassed with ruin, and he remained twisting and turning his hands over what he had spent on his property, which had now tumbled to pieces to its very foundations. And he could only say, 'Woe is me! Would I had never ascribed partners to my Lord and Cherisher!'* [5]

Be absolutely convinced that good actions will lead one to Paradise, not a sense of entitlement or guarantee. You have to truly seek out the pleasure of Allah and His mercy to win it. The Prophetﷺ said, "No one shall enter Paradise by virtue of his deeds." The companions asked, "Not even you, Messenger of Allah?" He answered, "Not even me—only by virtue of Allah immersing me in His mercy and favor."[6]

The greatest of the companions, may Allah be pleased with them, never had the feeling of having 'made it' in their journey of self-purification. Instead, they feared the punishment of Allah and sought His mercy with tireless, persistent effort. How can we presume to be better than them?

Knowledge must pair with action in order to be effective in defeating vanity. Remind yourself constantly of the blessings of Allah and the abilities that He gave you. What would you be without Him? Remind yourself that all of your blessings are yours only through His beneficence, not your ingenuity. You can preserve those blessings by constantly showing gratitude and using those abilities in the

5 The Quran, 14:42.
6 Bukhari and Muslim.

service of Allah. Remind yourself that you are not the only person on the earth with outstanding abilities and talents. There are many like you — and some who are certainly better than you. Whatever vanity coaxes you to do, do the opposite. If you feel vanity leading you to arrogance, strive to attain humility and perform those actions that bring humility to your heart. If vanity tempts you to feel overly confident and superior in your opinions, then work to seek the counsel of others, listen carefully to their words, and accept their good advice. If vanity causes you to look down on others and see them as below you, then realize that Allah is All-Powerful and can dispose of you as He chooses. Such thoughts will encourage you to be merciful and humble before others.

Self-Deception
Ghuroor literally means illusion or deception. When it refers to an aspect of human character, it can take on a variety of forms. Ghuroor as a trait is best described as self-deception or a false sense of security.

Some may be fooled by this temporary life and run after its false promises. All of their actions revolve around securing a place in this world and enjoying its immediate gratification. The Hereafter is distant in their minds, too far to warrant much thought or effort. This self-deception may also be with respect to Allah's blessings and mercy. Sometimes, a Muslim who indulges in sinning develops a false sense of security towards Allah's forgiveness. She delays her repentance, telling herself that there is always tomorrow, and reminds herself that Allah is forgiving. She forgets that although the mercy of Allah is vast and encompassing, His punishment is severe.

Another may feel overconfident in his good deeds, marveling at how much he has accumulated and believing that a passage to Heaven is guaranteed. This false sense of security may lead such a young Muslim to a leisurely, relaxed approach to serving Allah. This way of thinking can lead to neglect and blindness towards one's faults. A believer may also develop a false sense of security in her knowledge, wealth, status, or health. She feels certain that such blessings will be with her for the rest of her life. However, it is impossible to enjoy something forever in this life, and it is inevitable that those blessings will someday slip away.

This self-deception can be overcome with two elements: knowledge and action. Know that Allah is All-Powerful and capable of anything. Know the infiniteness of His power and the precision and perfection of His laws. He is the only refuge and the only real source of security. Such knowledge of Allah will help you avoid harboring delusions in this life.

Everything will one day vanish. Our families, our homes, cars, possessions, and friends will all be nothing. All of our hopes will turn to the Hereafter, and we will wonder if Allah will allow us to enter into His bliss. If He is not pleased with us, we are doomed.

A young Muslim who internalizes this belief will find it easier to focus her efforts on working for the Hereafter and will not become too secure in the delusions of this life. She will realize that by herself, she is nothing—it is the blessings of Allah that makes her what she is and what she is capable of. She will realize that the ultimate investment is in the Hereafter. There lies the true source of enjoyment, security, and contentment.

The action required to rectify self-deception is similar to that of vanity: do the opposite of what your desires whisper. If you feel a tendency to delay repentance, or feel secure in your future of the Hereafter, race, with all your being and effort, to forgiveness and good actions. Be extra-conscious of the Hereafter in all of your actions and thoughts. Remember that there are no guarantees and no one knows what Allah has in store for them—all that we can do is strive truly and sincerely for His pleasure.

Arrogance

Arrogance is to look down on others, believing oneself to be superior. A person with this fault of character may view others with scorn, derision, or disapproval. Usually, this person is also egotistic and blinded to the truth. Allah says, {Truly Allah knows what they hide and what they manifest; surely He does not love the arrogant.}[1]

The Prophet🙵 said, "One who has an atom's weight of arrogance in his heart will not enter heaven." A man asked, "But what if someone likes to wear fine clothes and shoes?" The Prophet🙵 said, "Allah is Beautiful, and He loves beauty. Arrogance is to disregard the truth and hold others in contempt."[2]

Arrogance is a consequence of vanity. Vanity, when allowed to escalate unchecked, leads a person to marvel at her own knowledge, intellect, appearance, strength, or other personal characteristics. Unchecked vanity will eventually lead her to hold herself superior to others.

1 The Quran, 16:23.
2 Muslim.

Degrees of Arrogance

The highest degree, and the most appalling, is arrogance in front of Allah. A person with this arrogance would not be considered a Muslim and could be counted among the likes of the Pharaoh at the time of Prophet Moses. Instead of submitting to their Creator, such people believe they are above worshipping a God.

The second degree of arrogance is towards the prophets of Allah. This arrogance is evident in the verses that tell us of the deeds of the Pharaoh and the disbelievers in his company: ❴They said: 'Shall we believe in two men like ourselves? And their people are slaves to us!'❵[3] A person who harbors this arrogance is also a disbeliever, as in the first degree.

The third degree of arrogance is towards people. There are many levels and manifestations of this arrogance, so we will only mention a few examples here. An individual who is arrogant towards her peers may turn her face away from people, ignoring them or pretending they are beneath her notice. Or she may cast them a look of disgust, as if they were inferior. This individual feels a rush of pleasure and self-satisfaction when people recognize her, stand to greet her in gatherings, or offer her their services.

Anas, may Allah be pleased with him, said, "There was no one more beloved to [the companions] than Allah's Messenger, peace be upon him, and yet they did not stand for him when they saw him, for they knew how he hated that."[4] It is acceptable, and even recommended, however, to stand and honor someone who deserves your respect, such as your parents, a just leader, or a righteous person. Standing to greet someone may be a recommended courtesy, but the individual who is being shown the respect should dislike such gestures and feel that such courtesy is unnecessary for them. It is when the respectful

3 The Quran, 23:47.
4 Tirmidhi.

gestures are relished by the recipient that there are probable scars of arrogance in his heart.

Another sign of arrogance towards people is manifested in the way one dresses, walks, speaks, or carries himself. He believes himself superior because of his privileged station, wealth, reputation, or level of education. Advice is not received well because this individual is confident he knows best and rarely seeks advice in the first place. Housework, laundry and other menial chores are beneath him. Such a person may believe that he is saved and privileged—that he 'has it made'—and that others are lost or doomed. The Prophetﷺ said, "If you hear a man say, 'Others are destroyed,' he is the one who is most destroyed."[5]

As we well know, the solution to character faults such as arrogance lies in knowledge and action. In terms of knowledge, the arrogant person should realize her true nature. She was created from a miniscule drop of liquid, which was created from mud, and will one day be reduced to dry dust, eaten by the bacteria and worms of the earth. Her body is like every human body, containing waste and blood. How can such a creature believe herself superior to others? If the source of arrogance is wealth, privilege, knowledge, or some other material resource, then he should know that it is all temporary, and can be snatched away at any moment.

Know that Allah is All-Capable. Only He is the source of strength, mightiness, and greatness. Allah says in a hadith qudsi[6], "Greatness is My attire and glory is My cloak. Whoever disputes Me in those, I will shatter him." Know the terrible punishment that awaits those who are arrogant. The Prophetﷺ said, "Shall I describe to you the people of Hell? They are the insolent, stingy, and arrogant ones."[7]

5 Muslim.
6 A saying of the Prophet in which he conveys something that Allah said.
7 Agreed upon.

Long for the reward of those who are humble. Their reward in the Hereafter is as Allah says, ❴That Home of the Hereafter We shall give to those who intend not high-handedness or mischief on earth: and the end is for the righteous.❵[8] And in this world, their reward is as the Messenger☀ described, "No one humbles himself before Allah but that he is elevated."

In terms of action, practice the opposite of what you may be tempted to do. Mingle with the poor or homeless, eat with them, and serve them. Take care of your own needs and help your family members with household chores. Be moderate in your attire and accept advice graciously. Practice humility in your speech, gait, and attitude. Accept the truth no matter how bitter it might taste. These practical tips, as well as many others, can help us discard any arrogance and instill humility in its place with the help of Allah.

8 The Quran, 28:83.

Part II
Instilling Good Character

The second method of personal development is to replace immoral habits with upright, good character. There are several general guidelines to keep in mind as we work to instill good characteristics.

Good character is the result of strong faith in Allah. As you work to improve aspects of your character, remember that you must simultaneously work on your relationship with Allah. As your faith increases or decreases your character will reflect a likewise change, for faith and character are inextricably connected.

Instill good characteristics that will overcome your weaknesses. If you have identified envy as your vulnerability, then engage in praying for those whom you envy, helping them, growing closer to them, and wanting the best for them. If arrogance is the weakness, then seek out tasks that you once avoided. Mingle in humility with people whom you previously scorned, pass out flyers, and clean the bathroom floors. Jump to take on behind-the-scenes jobs in Islamic work and go out of your way to help the classmate who is struggling desperately to keep up.

Repetition is essential to instilling good character. The Prophetﷺ taught us that patience and an even temper can be achieved through consistent effort and repetition. Just as we learned to write as children by scrawling letters over and over, drawing one backwards and one under the line, we must similarly teach ourselves good character through determined, patient practice.

Finally, as in the first step, good mentors and righteous friends will encourage us to improve our character. Spending time in such company is like being around a perfume seller—he will probably give you a sampling of his goods, but even if he does not, you will leave his company smelling good.

Repentance

Repentance is deep remorse after wrongdoing and a longing to return to a state of purity. This feeling is accompanied by a resolve never to return to the sin and a renewed determination to improve oneself. This combination of remorse and determination to return to Allah is called tawbah in Arabic.

Repentance to Allah is a constant duty because there are so many instances when we commit a sin with our limbs, have sinful thoughts, or spend our time ignorant of the presence of Allah. Allah says, ﴿And O Believers! Turn all of you together towards Allah, that you may attain Bliss.﴾[1] Prophet Muhammadﷺ said, "O people! Return to Allah and seek His forgiveness, for He forgives one hundred times, every single day."[2]

Repentance from Major and Minor Sins

Sins come in many forms and sizes—there are some that we regret deeply and others that we might think to dismiss lightly. There are major sins and minor sins and some that we don't even notice, but we must repent for all of them. Major sins are like an ambush lying

1 The Quran, 24:31.
2 Muslim

in wait for us if we do not make sincere repentance for them now. Someone who commits a major sin has a severe punishment awaiting him in the Hereafter if he did not bear its prescribed punishment in this life. In the latter case, the penalty received in this life takes the place of any punishment in the Hereafter.

Ibn Umar, may Allah be pleased with him, declared that there are seven types of major sins. He based his conclusion on the sound hadith: "'Beware of the seven destroyers." The companions asked, "And what are they, Messenger of Allah?" He answered, "Associating equals with Allah, practicing magic, murder, dealing in interest, confiscating the property of orphans, fleeing from the battlefield, and slandering virtuous, believing women." Abu Talib Al-Makki said that there are 17 major sins. He based his conclusion on many texts and ahadith. The 17 major sins that he listed are:

1. Four of the heart: associating partners with Allah, persistent sinning, despairing of Allah's mercy, and believing oneself beyond the punishment of Allah.

2. Four of the tongue: false testimony in a court, slandering believing women, swearing about something untrue, and practicing magic.

3. Three of the stomach: drinking alcohol, consuming the property or wealth of an orphan, and consuming interest.

4. Two of the hand: Murder and stealing.

5. One of the feet: fleeing from the battlefield.

6. One of all the limbs: ill-treatment of parents.

Minor sins encompass all that is not included in major sins, and they will be punished with a penalty in the Hereafter as well. These sins do not have prescribed punishments in this life unless they are repetitive and clearly harmful to others. If the penalty for these minor sins is received in this life, it is possible that one will actually receive reward in the Hereafter if she ceased the bad habit.

It is possible for minor sins to transform into major ones and become a source of much regret. This can take place in any of the following situations.

1. *When one persists with his sin.* The Prophetﷺ said, "A major sin is no longer major after seeking forgiveness, and a minor sin is no longer minor if it is persistent."[3]

2. *The sin is committed flagrantly.* The Prophet said, "All of my ummah[4] will be spared, except for those who commit sins flagrantly. An example of one who commits sins flagrantly is a man who sins at night, then wakes up after Allah had kept his sin hidden from the eyes of people. He says to another, "Last night, I did such and such." Thus, he spent the night with Allah covering him, but woke up exposing what Allah had covered."[5]

3. *Believing oneself safe from the punishment of Allah.* Someone who frequently commits minor sins may begin to believe, since the punishment of Allah has not yet befallen her, that Allah is not paying attention or that she will gain His forgiveness in the end. Thus, she no longer repents and begs His pardon. This is a serious error in understanding; it is possible that Allah may let someone go without punishment in order that she increases in her sins, because of His anger with such a person.

4. *The sinner is a person of understanding and knowledge.* It is vital that someone who is emulated as a scholar or a role-model not commit sins. If this person commits a sin, as we are all human, he should not speak of it and instead cover it with the veil of privacy that Allah provides. Of course, such a Muslim must repent immediately.

---

3 Tabarani.
4 Commonly translated as 'nation', the Muslim ummah refers to the collective population of Muslims, across time and space.
5 Bukhari and Muslim.

The conditions of Repentance

In order for repentance to be accepted by Allah, if He wills, you must satisfy four conditions.

1. *Remorse.* This is a deep ache in the heart due to whatever sin you have committed. Prophet Muhammadﷺ said, "Remorse is repentance."[6] A sin might actually lead someone to Paradise because it led him to repent, reform, and increase in his remembrance of Allah. The opposite is true—a good deed may lead someone to the wrath of Allah because the deed led him to self-admiration and negligence in improving himself.

2. *Stop performing the sin and seek forgiveness.* Ibn Umar narrates that the Prophetﷺ used to seek forgiveness one hundred times in a single gathering, saying, "O Lord, forgive me and accept my repentance, for you are Oft-Accepting of repentance, Merciful."[7] If the Prophet was so devoted in seeking forgiveness, what about us? The Prophetﷺ also said,

> For the one who regularly seeks Allah's forgiveness, Allah will give him relief from every worry, a way out from every impasse. He will give him provision from places he never expected.[8]

3. *Determination never to repeat the sin again.* A sincere resolve never to commit the sin again is a necessary condition for repentance. This resolve should not be half-hearted, but genuine. The question that comes to our minds is: what if we do repeat the sin? We are human and we are likely to surrender to our desires a second or third time, despite a firm resolve not to do so. If it happens, despite sincere determination, then once again seek forgiveness immediately and renew that strong resolve.

6 Al-Hakim: sahih.
7 Tirmidhi: Hasan sahih.
8 Abu Dawud.

These three preceding conditions are the right of Allah on you. As His servants, these are our obligations to Him after we commit a sin. However, for sins that violate the rights of other people, there is one more condition that must be fulfilled for the repentance to be accepted.

4. *Rectifying any wrong committed towards others.* This is the case whether the wrong was committed against human life, someone's property, honor, or feelings. If someone was killed by mistake, the penalty described in Surah An-Nisa' must be fulfilled.[9] If a Muslim killed another intentionally, then he must surrender himself to the family or guardian of the victim. If the family chooses, they may request that the prescribed punishment of death be applied by an Islamic court. If they wish, they may instead demand monetary compensation or simply forgive the perpetrator. If the latter two options are chosen, the sinner must still pay the reparations dictated in the verse of Surah An-Nisa.

If a Muslim commits adultery, steals, drinks alcohol, or perpetrates a sin in which there is a prescribed punishment in the Quran, he does not have to confess the sin publicly or turn himself in for his repentance to be accepted. Rather, he should shield himself with the curtain of privacy that Allah cast over him. Allah is The One who covers the sin and likes that sin to remain concealed. The only exception to this is murder; the murderer must surrender himself in order for his repentance to be accepted.

When a sin other than murder is openly confessed and is referred to an authority, it is then necessary to apply the prescribed punishment, if there is one in the Quran. If the individual is remorseful, the application of the punishment ensures that the repentance is acceptable to Allah and that there will be no punishment for it in the Hereafter.

9 The Quran, 4:92.

The evidence for these guidelines lie in the story of Ma'iz ibn Malik, who came to the Prophetﷺ to confess his sin. Ma'iz said, "O Messenger of Allah, I have wronged myself and committed adultery. I want you to purify me!" The Prophet turned away from him, giving him the option of reconsidering and resorting to the norm, which is to hide his sin from others. Ma'iz returned the next day and said, "Messenger of Allah, I committed adultery." The Prophet turned away from him again, so that he would reconsider his confession.

When Ma'iz approached him for the third time, asking to be punished, the Prophet ordered that a hole be dug in the ground and that the man be stoned to death. People were of two companies after the punishment—some said, "Ma'iz was destroyed and defeated by his sin." Others said, "There is no repentance as sincere as his." The Prophetﷺ then said, "He has made such repentance that if it were distributed over an entire nation, it would have sufficed it."[10] This is an example of someone who yearned so much for purification that he was willing to undergo severe punishment in order to guarantee freedom from the sin in the Hereafter. However, it is preferred to hide the sin and hope that Allah accepts the individual's repentance.

If someone took money unjustly, it should be returned to its owner if possible. If the owner is unknown, or the unlawful money is in the form of interest, the Muslim should do his best to estimate the amount of unlawful money. Then, he should give it to charity, hoping, with this deed, that Allah in His mercy accepts the sincere repentance, even though as a general rule only lawful money is accepted as charity.

When a Muslim harms another through her actions or speech, she should apologize and seek forgiveness from the person. However, if directly addressing the one who has been wronged would do more

10 Muslim.

good than harm, then it is better only to treat the wronged person well by strengthening the relationship and making dua for her.

Finally, when the wrongs committed are too many to count, the injustices too numerous to keep track of, or the wronged people have either died or moved away, there is no option except to beg forgiveness for oneself and for the people who were treated unjustly. Such a Muslim should increase his good actions so that they may compensate for the debts owed on the Day of Judgment.

On that Day, the people who were treated unjustly will take from the good deeds of such a Muslim. If his good deeds are depleted before all the injustices are rectified, the people who were wronged will begin to dump their bad deeds on his scale. Thus, the best course of action for such a person is to exert all effort in accumulating good deeds to prepare for that day. Allah says in the Quran, ‹Good deeds remove evil deeds.›[11] The Prophetﷺ said, "Be aware of Allah wherever you are and follow up the bad deed with a good one to erase it."[12]

Ways to Frequent Repentance
The primary reason young Muslims neglect seeking repentance are ignorance and laziness. Ignorance stems from believing that life is long and that there is always another chance. When we believe this, we procrastinate, busy ourselves with our daily life, and forget that death can come unexpectedly. The solution to ignorance is to learn about repentance and how essential it is to the believer's heart. Learn, also, of the punishment in store for someone who persists in his sins until death. The more we persist in a sin and delay repentance, the harder it is to be rid of it.

11 The Quran, 11:114.
12 Tirmidhi: Sahih.

Laziness and reluctance pose the second obstacle to frequent, earnest repentance. It can be overcome by strong willpower and self-control. A Muslim should probe his heart to discover why he might resist repentance. This self-discipline and self-awareness is obtained with the help of Allah and reliance on Him. Occupying oneself with good deeds and positive habits, such as reading, seeking knowledge, activism, and exercise, is also encouragement for frequent repentance.

The Outcome of Repentance on the Day of Judgment

What will become of a Muslim who committed a major sin, was not punished in this life, but repented sincerely and fulfilled all of the conditions of repentance? She will meet Allah as if she had never committed such a deed, as the Prophet promised. Heﷺ said, "The one who repents sincerely from a sin becomes as one who never committed it."[13] She is just as a soiled cloth that was washed, rinsed, and cleansed of any traces of stains. The heart is pure and untainted.

As for the Muslim who avoided major sins and intermittently fell into various minor sins, none of which were persistent but for which he did not repent, it is possible that those sins will be covered up and forgiven. Allah says in the Quran, ﴾If you shun the great sins which you are forbidden, We will do away with your small sins and admit you through a gate of great honor.﴿[14] This verse should not lead you to neglect seeking forgiveness for the smaller sins, for repentance will increase your good deeds and soften your heart. The Messengerﷺ sought forgiveness one hundred times a day, even though he did not commit sins, large or small.

The fate that we all dread is meeting death before we repent for our sins. That is indeed a grave situation. If Allah wishes, He will forgive. If He wishes, He will punish. The events and dealings on the Day of

13 At-Tabarani.
14 The Quran, 4:31.

Judgment are only partially revealed to us. There are many unknown and astounding aspects of that Day that we are incapable of foreseeing. Someone who committed mountains of sins might be forgiven while another who amassed so many obvious good deeds could be punished due to the heart's condition. There is also the element of God-consciousness[15], a factor that can only be measured by The All-Knowing Creator.

Levels of Seeking Repentance

The highest level is that of a believer who persists with repentance throughout her life. This believer may have a few minor shortcomings in her daily habits, but very few deliberate sins. This person is one whom the Quran calls the "racer to good." Her repentance is called "the sincere tawbah" and her soul is called "the serene soul", as described in the Quran.

Almost equal to the first level is a believer who repents constantly throughout his life. He commits sins but is quick to seek forgiveness. This believer is also of high rank and is promised pardon from Allah: ⟨Those who avoid great sins and shameful deeds, only falling into small faults—verily thy Lord is ample in forgiveness.⟩[16]

A lower level of repentance is of one who repents frequently for most of his sins. However, there are one or two desires that overwhelm him and cause him to persist in sinning. After these sins, this Muslim is filled with regret and seeks forgiveness and hopes that Allah would spare him. If this Muslim is dedicated to good actions and detests falling into sin, it can be hoped that he will fall into the category described in this verse,

15 Taqwa, which means being God-conscious, God-fearing, and filled with awe and
   humility before Allah.
16 The Quran, 53:32.

{ Others there are who have acknowledged their wrongdoings: they have mixed righteous action with evil actions. Perhaps Allah will turn to them in Mercy: for Allah is Oft-Forgiving, Merciful. } [17]

However, if he falls into the trap of procrastinating and delaying repentance, he is in much danger. He may be snatched by death before he repents. In that case, Allah will decide whether to forgive or punish.

The lowest level of one who practices repentance is one who repents and then returns full-heartedly to the sin for which she repented, without reminding herself of her former resolve. She is of those who are insistent upon their sins, and her soul is one that the Quran describes as "driven by evil." Such a person should be extremely fearful that she may die while she is in such a state of disobedience to Allah.

17 The Quran, 9:102.

Pure Intentions, Sincerity, and Forthrightness with Allah

Intentions

The intention, An-Niyyah, is the purpose that lies behind our actions. Whoever wishes to win the pleasure of Allah, His reward, and His Paradise will profit and succeed in his actions. And whoever aims to please people, seeking their approval and notice, will gain nothing. As for the Muslim who neglects to make a conscious intention in his actions, he exerted energy and time in an action that will reap nothing. The Prophetﷺ said in a sahih hadith,

> Actions are but by intentions. Every one will get what they intended. So whoever migrates for the sake of Allah and His messenger, his migration will truly be for the sake of Allah and His messenger. And whoever migrates for the sake of an increase in worldly benefit or to marry someone, his migration will be for the sake of whatever he migrated for.

Mundane actions can become worship if they are driven by a worthy intention. Eating, for example, becomes an act of worship if the intention is to gather strength to serve Allah. Marriage can be an act of worship if the intention is to shield oneself from sin and to build a righteous Muslim society. Wearing perfume can be an act of worship if you intend to follow the sunnah of the Prophet and to prevent bad odors that might repel people. Studying and working towards a college degree can be an act of worship if the intention is to serve Allah with your knowledge, to teach others, and to better the human condition. As the preceding examples illustrate, an action can be either a routine step in life or a noble act of worship, depending on the intention.

The Prophet said, "Even intercourse can be charity."[1] This hadith demonstrates that a seemingly neutral personal habit, such as intercourse with one's spouse, is rewarded if the intention is right. For example, if a person intends to fulfill his desire through means that Allah has made permissible to His servants or to procreate righteous children the action is transformed into a righteous and noble deed.

A righteous intention elevates a person, regardless of whether the action was actually performed. The Prophet said, "Whoever truly asks Allah for martyrdom, Allah will count him among the ranks of the martyrs, even while he is on his deathbed, suffering a natural death."[2] He also said, speaking during the campaign of Tabuk, "You have left behind in Madinah men who, for every valley you cross and every path you take [on this campaign], they share in your reward—for they were detained only because of illness."[3] Finally, he said in one more hadith, "Whoever intends to do a good deed, but did not perform it, will have a reward recorded for him."[4] However, if the action is actually performed, the Muslim may receive anywhere from ten times to 700 times the reward, or much, much more.

A single action can reap multiple rewards and count as multiple actions, if it is motivated by more than one good intention. For ex-

1 Muslim.   3 Bukhari and Muslim.
2 Muslim.   4 Bukhari and Muslim.

ample, a young Muslim praying congregational prayer in the mosque may have several intentions: to fulfill the obligation of prayer, to observe the sunnah of congregational prayer, to get to know and help his brothers in Islam, and increase in knowledge. These various motivations will result in multiplied rewards. Similarly, someone who owns a business can have the intention of working to build and contribute to society and the world, providing for his family through just means, and calling others to Islam through the relationships and reputation that he builds in his business. You can develop multiple intentions for almost any good deed that you perform, in order to reap increased reward insha'allah.

It is important to remember that a sin does not become a good action because of a good intention. A Muslim should not steal with the intention of giving to the poor, for example. He may not commit acts of violence against the innocent in order to advocate a just cause. In Islam, the end does not justify the means. Rather, a noble goal must be achieved through equally noble means.

The intention is an action of the heart and summoning it before every action is not always easy. It takes practice and patience—constantly renewing and revisiting intentions throughout the entire day, everyday. An intention can transform from seeking the pleasure of Allah to seeking the approval of people in an instant, without your notice. Thus, it is vital to exercise constant watchfulness and awareness of your own heart. Someone who succeeds with her intentions, accompanying every action with a noble intention to please Allah, transforms her entire life into worship. She has come closer to embodying the purpose of life, as Allah says, ❴I have not created jinn[5] or people except to worship Me.❵[6]

---

5 One of Allah's creations that were also granted free will and will be held
  accountable for their actions on the Day of Judgment.
6 The Quran, 51:56.

Sincerity

Sincerity ensures that the action is not only good and preceded by some good intentions, but that it is totally for Allah. It is possible for someone to have good intentions to please Allah, but they are mixed with some other motives. Allah says in the Quran, ⟨And they have been commanded no more than this: To worship Allah, offering Him sincere devotion, being true in faith; to establish regular prayer; and to practice regular charity; and that is the Religion, straight and true.⟩[7] Anything good may possibly be tainted with mixed intentions. When a heart is pure and completely free of any mixed intentions, then it is has achieved ikhlas, or sincerity.

The chapter on Riya in Part I is central to understanding the nature of sincerity. It offers advice on how to avoid falling into the trap of seeking the approval and admiration of people.

Being Forthright and Truthful with Allah

> ⟨Among the Believers are men who have been true to their covenant with Allah. Of them, some have completed their vow (through martyrdom) and some still wait, but they have never the least faltered in their determination.⟩[8]

These words from the Quran alert us to the centrality of truthfulness in Islam. Our relationship with our Creator should be founded on candor and honesty. The Prophetﷺ said,

> Truthfulness leads to piety, and piety leads to Paradise. A man will keep telling the truth until it will be written in heaven that he is a 'truthful one.' Lying leads to shameless-

7 The Quran, 98:5.
8 The Quran, 33:23.

ness, and shamelessness leads to Hell. A man will keep telling lies, until one day it will be written that he is a 'liar.'[9]

Our truthfulness and forthrightness before Allah is manifested in
several ways, some of which are described here:

  1. *Sincere motivation.* The aim behind our every action should be
Allah and only Him. We should not be deceitful or dishonest before
Allah, for He sees that which is in our hearts. The hypocrites at the
time of the Prophetﷺ used to swear that Muhammad was the Messenger of Allah, but Allah revealed, ⟨Allah witnesses that the hypocrites are liars.⟩[10] Thus, although the words they spoke were true,
their hearts were so fraudulent that Allah exposed them as liars.

  2. *Truthful speech.* The Muslim should speak the absolute truth, be
faithful to his promises, and always testify to the truth even when it
may implicate himself or others. The Quran commands, ⟨O you who
believe! Stand out firmly for justice, as witnesses to Allah, even against
yourselves, your parents, or your kin, and whether it be against rich
or poor: for Allah can best protect both.⟩[11] Lying and double-deal-
ing while buying and selling is common in modern society, but the
Prophetﷺ expressly forbade it.

  3. *Determination in carrying out our duties.* When we promise ourselves that we will stand up for Islam and for justice, responding to
the call of jihad be it within ourselves, educating our community,
or physically defending the oppressed, we should be determined
to fulfill that promise. We should not be people of weak determination and unkept promises. Excuses, half-completed tasks, and
apologies should rarely be our resort. Rather, when we commit to a
responsibility in our personal lives or in our Islamic work, we should

9 Agreed upon.
10 The Quran, 63:1.
11 The Quran, 4:135.

be determined to deliver to our utmost ability in the most excellent possible manner.

4. Constancy in all situations. A Muslim activist's willpower must not be swayed by his circumstances and life situation. If he intended to do some good during a time of prosperity, his willpower should not be deterred by an unexpected obstacle. Highly relevant to the topic of unshakable will is a story told by Anas ibn Malik about his uncle, Anas ibn An-Nadr, both companions of the Prophet. Anas ibn An-Nadr missed the Battle of Badr, because, like several others, he did not realize that there would be a confrontation with the leaders of Makkah. Anas was so disappointed at missing the great moment that he said to himself, "The first battle encounter with the Messenger of Allah—and I missed it! But by Allah, if I get another chance to join a battle with the Messenger of Allah, Allah will witness what I will do!"

On the day of the Battle of Uhud, when there was confusion within the Muslim ranks and some had begun to retreat, Sa'd ibn Mu'adh narrated that he saw Anas ibn An-Nadr charging toward the enemy by himself, a single, resolute warrior. Sa'd called out to him, "Where are you going all by yourself?" Anas answered, "I smell the winds of Paradise! I feel their scent coming from Mount Uhud." Anas fought singly until he was killed—when his body was found it was covered with more than 80 sword blows and arrows. His sister could only identify him by looking at a scar on one of his fingers, which she recognized. It was on this occasion that the verse was revealed, {Among the Believers are men who have been true to their covenant with Allah.}[12]

---

12 The narration is by Tirmidhi and is Sahih.

5. *Truthful in Action.* Someone who practices truthfulness should find that their outward appearance reflects their inward state. There are no hidden feelings lying under a façade of calm—the Muslim is upfront and open. The Muslim should work towards practicing forthrightness in all of her actions and manners. When a young Muslims' heart is filled with trust in Allah, sincerity, taqwa, fear of Allah, and hope for His pleasure, she will find her compelling inner state reflected in her outward dealings. This reflection is not to impress people or invoke their admiration; it should be purely for the sake of the Creator.

Patience

⟨ Those who patiently persevere will truly receive a reward without measure!⟩[1]

The Prophetﷺ said, "No one is given a better, more expansive gift than patience."[2] Patience is a cherished attribute because it helps a person to be steadfast on the journey to Allah's pleasure and His Paradise. Prophet Muhammadﷺ said, "Patience to faith is like the head to a body."[3] He also said in another hadith,

> How remarkable is the situation of the believer! His situation is always good, which is the case only with the believer. If he is blessed with prosperity, he is thankful and that is good for him. If he is tested with difficulty, he is patient and that is also good for him.[4]

There are different kinds of patience, and each human being may find that one type comes naturally to him and another must be strived for. Patience can be the ability to endure physical hard-

---

1 The Quran, 39:10.
2 Bukhari, Muslim.
3 Bukhari, Muslim.
4 Muslim.

ship with patience. This type of patience includes persevering in acts of worship that require physical strength, such as Hajj, fasting, and spending long hours working in the service of Allah. Patience can be dealing well with people or persisting in good habits. There is also internal patience—perseverance in disciplining the self. This kind of patience may include resisting desires, persistence in self-improvement, and the determination to defeat a bad habit.

Patience and perseverance take on many familiar names, depending on their context. Patience in the battlefield may be called courage and patience with physical desires may be called chastity. The subject that we are examining in this chapter includes the many forms and contexts of patience and perseverance, which in our language one word alone cannot encompass.

Categories of Patience

In this chapter, we will examine three areas in which patience is exercised. These three areas include: perseverance in acts of obedience, patience in resisting sin, and patience in times of affliction. The first two categories contain greater reward than the third, because they are a matter of choice and willpower while the third is not.

1. *Perseverance in acts of obedience.* Our desires naturally resist being steadfast in acts of obedience. We may feel lazy to wake up to pray and hesitant when it is time to give charity. We may feel apprehensive at the moment when we must stand up and defend the truth. That is why good deeds must be accompanied by patience and willpower before, during, and after the act. Patience before the action means summoning all of the good intentions and striving to purify them from ulterior motives. It means fighting off the whispers of the shaitan as he tries to dissuade you from carrying out a good action.

Patience during the action involves perfecting its performance and continuing the struggle of purifying intentions. It also entails keeping your energy, focus, and steadfastness throughout the performance of the action. Patience after the deed can involve not mentioning it to others for the sake of praise or approval.

Another form of patience is resisting too much indulgence in worldly pleasures, even though those pleasures may be permissible. Such self-control requires a large measure of patience and persistence. When we allow ourselves to become too immersed in worldly pleasures we become numb, unaware of the state of our heart and unable to part with the joys we indulge in. This leads to weakness and immoderation, and eventually to sin. Allah says, ⁅Know that your possessions and your children are but a trial; and that your highest reward lies with Allah.⁆[5]

Abdurahman ibn Awf, a famous companion of the Prophet, once said, "We were tested with affliction, and we were patient. We were then tested with prosperity, but we were not patient." It is easy to fall in the trap that he describes because we are alert in tests of affliction, but may be slower to realize that prosperity may be a test as well. We sometimes forget to summon patience and perseverance in times of ease.

The best way to endure a difficulty is to prepare yourself for it, persevere, and be patient. As for the test of prosperity, it is a slippery one that will conquer all except those who are living with the Hereafter in their minds. Those individuals will be alert to the deception of pleasure and ease. Some of the righteous people have said, "The believer is patient in affliction. But no one is steadfast during prosperity except for the one who is ever-conscious of the Hereafter."

2. *Patience in resisting sin.* Keeping away from sin requires a high level of perseverance and patience, especially avoiding those sins that are prevalent such as gossip, white lies, and spreading rumors. The Prophetﷺ said, "The muhajir [the migrant for the sake of Allah] is

5 The Quran, 8:28.

the one who abandons evil, and the mujahid [the one who strives for Allah] is the one who fights his desires."[6]

In an environment such as ours, where sin and immorality are widespread, patience in resisting the environment around us takes strong will and a vitalizing faith. As Muslim activists, we should never go with the flow without making sure that the path is free of disobedience to Allah. The Prophetﷺ said,

> Do not be a follower, saying, 'I am with the people. If they do good, I will do good. If they do wrong, so will I.' Rather, brace yourselves!—so that when people do good, you do good, and when they commit evil, you refrain from their wrongdoing.[7]

Remember that exercising patience in this environment may lead you to a greater reward than if you were somewhere else or living in another era. Our environment is not an excuse to let go of our mission and lose our patience and steadfastness. Allah placed us in this time and place in order to serve Him and worship Him, here and now in 21st-century America.

3. *Patience in calamity.* During our lives, we may be stricken with calamities such as the death of a loved one, poverty, illness, and maltreatment at the hands of people. Allah says in the Quran,

> ❴ *Be sure we shall test you with something of fear and hunger, some loss in goods, lives, and the fruits of your toil, but give glad tidings to those who patiently persevere. Those who say, when afflicted with calamity, 'To Allah we belong, and to Him is our return'.* ❵[8]

---

6 Ibn Majah, An-Nisaa'i (second part).
7 Tirmidhi.
8 The Quran, 2:155-156.

The Prophetﷺ said,

Each and every thing that afflicts the Muslim of suffering, hardship, anxiety, sadness, harm, and distress, even a thorn that pricks him, will be a means for Allah to erase his sins.[9]

The Prophet also said about being patient when among people,

The Muslim who interacts with others and bears the aggravation in dealing with them is better than one who does not interact with people and cannot bear their shortcomings.[10]

Hoping for a calamity or a test from Allah, in order to test or prove the strength of your patience, is inappropriate for the believer. There is a hadith in which the Prophet said, "Seek refuge in Allah from the strain of calamity, the depths of suffering, misfortune, and the malicious enemy."[11] It is wrong to hope for a misfortune because we do not know whether we will be able to deal with it patiently nor whether we will end our life with the strong faith that we hope for.

Working to prevent calamities and taking precautions against misfortune through lawful means is an obligation upon every Muslim. It is wrong to leave things up to fate, thinking that we will be patient no matter what happens. The Muslim takes care of his affairs, works for his goals, and looks after the welfare of those whom he is responsible for. When things do not work out as planned or misfortune befalls him, it is then that he exercise patience. Prophet Muhammadﷺ ordered the early Muslims to migrate to Ethiopia in order to avoid affliction and to protect their faith. One of the righteous people once said,

9 Bukhari and Muslim.
10 Tirmidhi.
11 Bukhari and Muslim.

"To be in prosperity and thankful is better than being in affliction and exercising patience."

When difficulty does befall us, our motto should be "Patience is the best resort." Those were the words of Prophet Yaqub when he lost his son, Prophet Yusuf. All trust should be placed in Allah, who is our Protector and the Guardian of our affairs. He is the one who softens pain and gives comfort. When Prophet Ibrahim was thrown in the fire by his people, Allah made the fire a haven for him, ﴿[Allah] said: O fire, be a source of coolness and peace to Ibrahim.﴾[12]

Memorize and ponder these deep words of advice from Prophet Muhammadﷺ to a young teenager. Abdullah ibn Abbas said, "One day I was riding behind the Prophet and he said to me,

> Young man, I shall teach you some words of advice. Be mindful of Allah, and Allah will protect you. Be mindful of Allah, and you will find Him at your side. If you ask, ask of Allah. If you seek help, seek help from Allah. Know that if all people were to gather together to benefit you, they would benefit you only with something that Allah had already prescribed for you. And if they gather together to harm you, they would harm you only with something Allah had already prescribed for you. The pens have been lifted and the pages have dried.[13]

In another powerful narration, the Prophetﷺ said,

> Know Allah in times of prosperity, and you will find Him close to you in times of difficulty...Know that with patience comes victory, after suffering comes relief, and with difficulty comes ease.

12 The Quran, 21:69.
13 Tirmidhi.

The Etiquette of Patience

The Prophet instructed us on how to exercise patience in the best manner when a tragedy strikes. Below are four guidelines that should be implemented in order for patience to be achieved correctly.

1. *Be patient from the first moment* that calamity afflicts you or bad news reaches you. The Prophet said, "Patience is at the first shock of calamity."[14] This means that the young believer should always be in touch with her intentions and the state of her heart, so that if disaster hits, she can readily remember the purpose of her existence and the importance of patience. The Muslim should race to remember Allah and His reward for those who suffer, before the shaitan tempts her to lose her self-control.

One should never wish for that which did not happen, thinking, "If only I had done differently!" 'If only' opens the doors of regret, despair, and helplessness. These thoughts lead the Muslim to blame herself and lose the strength to remain patient. If there were some errors in judgment, it is important to contemplate them and learn from them so that they will not repeat themselves. However, this self-examination should not lead to despair. The Prophet said in an important hadith related to self-control and patience,

> The strong believer is better and more beloved to Allah than the weak believer, and in both lies goodness. Keenly pursue what benefits you, seek help from Allah, and do not fail. If something befalls you, do not say, "If only I had done such, things would be different" but rather say, "Whatever Allah wills will come to pass," for 'if only' unlocks the work of the shaitan.[15]

14 Agreed upon.
15 Muslim.

The Prophetﷺ used to seek refuge from weak resolve in a very powerful supplication that should be recited by all young Muslims who are active on the path of Allah. He used to say, "O Allah! I seek refuge from anxiety and sorrow, from despair and laziness, from cowardice and greed, and from the burden of debt and the mischief of people."[16]

2. *Remember immediately that everyone will return to Allah* at some point. Upon receiving news of a calamity, we should say, "Inna lillahi wa inna ilaihi raji'un,": To Allah we belong and to Him we return. The Prophetﷺ said,

> When a slave of Allah is afflicted with a difficulty and says, 'To Allah we belong and to Him we return. O Allah! Reward me in this trial, and bless me with what is better,' Allah will most surely reward him for his suffering and bless him with something better in place of what he lost.[17]

3. *Stay calm and in control.* One of the signs of perfected patience is that distress does not show on the one who is suffering. Such was the patience of Um Sulaym, may Allah be pleased with her, when her beloved child passed away. Abu Talha, her husband, was away and had not yet heard the news. When he returned in the evening, Um Sulaym adorned herself to greet him and helped her husband to relax and rest before she told him of the death of his son. She broke the news saying, "Our son was a trust from Allah, and Allah has taken him back again." Because of the gentle way in which his wife broke the news, Abu Talha was able to remember Allah and remain patient.

The next day, Abu Talha told the Prophet the story of how his wife had conducted herself, and the Prophetﷺ responded, "O Allah, bless them for that night." One person reported that many years lat-

---

16 Abu Dawud.
17 Muslim.

er, the couple had been blessed with seven children who all knew the Quran very well.[18]

It is natural to cry and feel grief when a loved one is lost or a sad event takes place. These expressions are not displeasure with the will of Allah—rather, they are signs of a tender and merciful heart. When Ibrahim, the infant son of Prophet Muhammad, passed away, his father's eyes overflowed with tears. The companions asked him about the crying: was it impatience with the will of Allah? The Prophet☺ replied, "This [crying] is just mercy."[19] He also said, "Allah shows mercy to His servants who are merciful."[20]

4. *Do not complain about your suffering.* It is better not to spread the details of your situation, in order to avoid complaining or inflaming the grief in your own heart. Such behavior may decrease your reward with Allah. However, sharing your situation with a close friend who may ease your burden, give you good counsel, and remind you of Allah is not complaining and is part of the Islamic bond of brotherhood.

How to Instill Patience in Yourself

Patience and perseverance are essential characteristics to instill in ourselves. However, they require discipline and hard work before they become innate aspects of our personality. They may be achieved through knowledge and persistent action.

Know the merits of patience and perseverance and understand how they help you to remain steadfast in the service of Allah. Know the consequences of not being patient—you may become lax and undisciplined in your Islamic work. You may fall into sin, become negligent, or be unable to control yourself in a calamity.

18 Muslim.
19 Bukhari and Muslim.
20 Tabarani.

In terms of action, you must work to instill patience gradually by taking small steps and increasing your actions over time. Practice resisting temptations and use your strong will to fight petty desires. Like a muscle in the body, you must exercise your willpower in order to strengthen it. There will come a time when your heart will rejoice in its ability to overcome trivial desires, instead of regretting the loss of pleasure. Many acts of worship can help increase patience, such as fasting, giving charity, and other disciplined acts. Occupy yourself with good, productive actions so that it is easier to persevere in avoiding what is forbidden.

Thankfulness

❴ What can Allah gain by your punishment, if you are grateful and you believe? Verily, it is Allah who recognizes all good, and knows all things. ❵[1]

Thankfulness to Allah is practiced through the heart, the tongue, and the body. Thankfulness of the heart is to be aware and appreciative of the blessings of Allah. Thankfulness of the tongue is to thank the Creator constantly, by speaking words of praise and thanks.

Thanking with the body is to use the blessings of Allah in His service. A sharp mind should be used in the pursuit of knowledge; the eyes should be used to contemplate, read, and work for Allah; wealth should be used to help people for the sake of Allah. So should every blessing be used to achieve the pleasure of Allah.

Thankfulness actually leads to an increase in your blessings. It is your route to growing closer to Allah, increasing the good things you have in this life, and ensuring that they are a source of reward and goodness. Allah says, ❴ If you are grateful, I will give you more. But if you show ingratitude, truly My punishment is terrible indeed. ❵[2]

1 The Quran, 4:147.
2 The Quran, 14:7.

There are many forms of thankfulness that we should strive to practice, some of which are described here. A young Muslim may feel embarrassed before Allah because she realizes His great bounty on her and her subsequent shortcomings in offering thanks. This individual has practiced a form of thankfulness to Allah. Realizing the grace and gentleness of Allah towards you and acknowledging how much you fall short in thanking Him is a form of gratefulness.

Using your blessings and talents for His sake is a form of thankfulness, as is being content with whatever Allah has given you. Thankfulness includes appreciating the smallest blessing. Thanking any human being who has helped you or given you something is a form of thankfulness to Allah. We know this because the Prophetﷺ said, "Whoever has not thanked people has not thanked Allah."[3]

Our beloved Prophet Muhammadﷺ expressed his thanks to Allah in the most beautiful ways. He used to pray at night until his feet swelled. Aishah asked him, "You do all of this, although Allah has forgiven all of your past and future sins?"

"Should I not be a thankful slave?" responded the Prophet.[4]

The Prophetﷺ also used to express his thanks to Allah by making the prostration of thankfulness. Abu Bakr said, "Whenever the Prophet received good news or was pleased by something, he would fall into prostration out of thankfulness."[5] The Prophetﷺ would do this whether or not he had wudu.

The Clear and Hidden Blessings of Allah

It is impossible to count or name all of the blessings that Allah has given us. Allah says, ﴿If you were to count the favors of Allah, never would you be able to number them.﴾[6] Some of those blessings, such

---

3 Tirmidhi: sahih.
4 Agreed upon.
5 Abu Dawud.
6 The Quran, 16:17.

as health, wealth, children, social status, and others, are obvious to any observer, even though we may not always appreciate them duly. Many are more subtle, such as the light of guidance, a wise, perceptive heart, contentment in life, the love of Allah, good character, and others. Finally, there are blessings that we rarely detect, and thus are often neglectful of, even though they are great blessings indeed.

Once, a wise, righteous Muslim entered into the presence of one of the ruling governors in the Islamic empire. The governor asked for some water. Upon this, the righteous man asked the governor, "If you had to trade the whole world for a glass of water, would you sacrifice the world?"

"Yes," the governor said.

"Then drink, and may Allah bless you."

Some time after the governor drank his water, the man asked again, "If you were unable to relieve yourself after drinking this water, and had to trade the whole world in order to expel the water from your body, would you do so?"

"Yes!" responded the governor.

"What do you think of the blessing of something that you would trade the whole world to have, and then trade the whole world to get rid of?" asked the man, demonstrating his point.

This story has many lessons in thankfulness. It illustrates how insignificant this world is, and yet, how necessary are a drink of water and the ability to relieve oneself. These are hidden blessings that we often neglect to appreciate.

Even Hardship is a Blessing

Realizing that hardship is a blessing is part of thankfulness. This realization is captured perfectly in the words of Umar ibn Al-Khattab, who said,

I have never been tested with a difficulty except that I have found myself thanking Allah the Almighty for four great blessings: That my faith was not weakened, that the test was not something more severe, that I was not deprived of the ability to be content and see the good in my situation, and that I can hope for reward due to the suffering I experienced.

Hope & Fear

Hope and fear intertwine in the heart of the believer. One cannot exist independently of the other, and they should balance one another depending upon the circumstances of the believer. Allah says, ❴Their sides forsake their beds, as they call on their Lord in fear and hope—and they spend out of the sustenance which We have given them.❵[1]

Aishah, may Allah be pleased with her, said, "I asked the Prophet, 'In the verse that says, ❴Those who give and their hearts quiver out of fear❵, does that refer to a man who steals and fornicates?' The Prophetﷺ answered, "No. It speaks of the man who fasts, prays, and gives charity, yet he fears that it may not be accepted from him."[2]

Fear and Awe

The fear we speak about here is anticipation of an impending calamity brought about by our own actions. We may fear the horrors of judgment, punishment in Hell-fire, torment in our graves, or displeasing Allah. As part of this fear, we also feel an overwhelming sense of awe as we recognize the greatness and breathtaking glory of Allah. Those most in awe of Allah will be those who have the deepest knowledge of

---

1 The Quran, 32:17.
2 Al-Hakim: sahih.

their Creator and of their own souls. The Prophetﷺ said, "I am the most fearful and most in awe of Allah."[3] The Quran tells us, ❴Those who truly fear Allah, among His Servants, are the ones who have knowledge. Allah is Exalted in Might, Forgiving.❵[4] We can infer from this that a practical step towards instilling this fear of Allah in our hearts is to expand our knowledge of Him.

There are several types of fear—some which we want to steer clear of. Positive fear is one that not only affects the heart, but translates into motivated action. It is not a desperate fear. It is coupled with awe, love, and a deep desire to grow closer to Allah. This fearful, awed heart is humble and tranquil, free from arrogance, bitterness, and envy. Its primary occupation is to improve itself and hold itself accountable in preparation for the trials of the Judgment Day. This constructive fear has positive effects in the form of action. The Muslim holds himself back from sinning and is disciplined in his worship in order to compensate for any shortcomings and to prepare for his Judgment before Allah.

Negative fear is very different. We should bar this fear from our hearts and minds. Negative fear is mixed with feelings of paralysis, helplessness, and despair. A fear that leaves a person paralyzed and unwilling to act, lest another mistake be committed, will lead to withdrawal from the arena of Islamic work. Fear that is mixed with despair may lead to embracing sin, because this person believes there is no hope for him anyway.

It is important to be well-acquainted with yourself in order to nurture positive fear and avoid a paralyzing fear. Different approaches to fear resound with different people—some people are sensitive to the slightest reminder while others need to envision Allah's punishment to create action-oriented fear. Some people fear dying before

---

3 Bukhari and Muslim.
4 The Quran, 35:28.

they have a chance to repent, and some people fear becoming too absorbed in worldly blessings.

Fear of becoming weak and losing faith is a call to action for some people, while others respond more to contemplation of the anguish of death or the punishment of the grave. Some people fear standing before Allah and being judged, and others fear plunging down for many years into Hell. Some hearts are inspired with awe and fear by observing creation: the night sky, the laws of physics, the human body. Because our hearts are different, we respond to diverse reminders and manners of giving advice.

How to Achieve Positive Fear and Defeat Paralyzing Fear
Positive fear can be instilled through knowledge and action. Know that Allah is Great, Merciful, and Forgiving, but also that He is severe in punishment. Allah says, ❴Say: O my Servants who have transgressed against their souls! Do not despair of the Mercy of Allah, for Allah forgives all sins—He is Oft-Forgiving, Most Merciful.❵[5] At the same time, in another verse Allah tells us these frightening words, ❴The Word from Me will come true: I will fill Hell with jinn and men all together.❵[6]

Know that the door to forgiveness is open at all times, but four conditions must be fulfilled in order to win that forgiveness.[7] Allah says, ❴But, without doubt, I am also He that forgives again and again, to those who repent, believe, and do right: those who are ready to receive true guidance.❵[8] Saving ourselves from destruction will come if we actualize the conditions described in Surah Al-Asr, ❴Verily mankind is at loss. Except for those who believe, do righteous deeds, and encourage one another in truth and patience.❵[9]

5 The Quran, 39: 28.
6 The Quran, 32:13.
7 See the chapter on Tawbah:
  Seeking Repentance.

8 The Quran, 20:82.
9 The Quran.

Know that your heart can change overnight. One might wake up in the morning full of faith and go to sleep with a heart that has come near to disbelief. Our hearts are between the fingers of Allah and He can reverse them as He wills. Because of this, the Prophet☵ used to supplicate, "O Allah, Who changes the hearts as He wills, set my heart firmly on obedience to you."[10]

Know also how much the Prophet☵ and his companions feared Allah, given their high level of faith and devotion. When the Prophet☵ prayed, a wheezing sound like the hissing of a teapot could be heard from his crying.[11] Aishah, may Allah be pleased with her, said that when the weather would become stormy, the Prophet's face would become anxious. He would pace the room, entering and leaving repeatedly, worried that Allah's punishment would befall his people.[12] Umar ibn Al-Khattab was known to hear verses that would shake him so severely that he would be ill for days. And the flow of tears down the cheeks of Ibn Abbas were said to leave constant marks on his face. These examples can inspire us to instill fear in our hearts and become more sensitive to the remembrance of Allah.

Know that fear leads to salvation from the punishment of Allah. Allah says in the Quran, ﴾And for he who fears standing before his Lord, there will be two gardens.﴿[13] The Prophet☵ said, "Two eyes will not be touched by the Fire: eyes that wept in fear of Allah, and eyes that spent the night on duty guarding for the sake of Allah."[14]

As always, this knowledge must be complemented by action. Remember that persistent sinning deadens the soul and reduces the sensitivity to remembrance of Allah. It makes the heart hard and the eyes dry. Increased worship, good deeds, and abstaining from sins will increase

10 Muslim.
11 Tirmidhi.
12 Agreed upon.
13 The Quran, 55:46.
14 Tirmidhi: hasan.

fear and sensitivity in the heart. Constant contemplation of the future and of Allah's creation will also increase this characteristic. A heart that contemplates deeply will know more about its Creator. When a soul knows its Creator, it will undoubtedly fear and love Him.

Hope

Hope for the mercy of Allah, His pleasure, and His Paradise should never be absent from the heart of the believer. No matter where you are in your life or what your level of faith is; no matter what you have done or how far you are from the straight path, there is always hope for returning to Allah.

Hope cannot exist in a vacuum. Hope must be accompanied by action upon which that hope can be based, such as good deeds and avoiding sin. When hope makes you feel overly secure and laid back in the struggle for self-improvement, it is a false hope. Allah says in the Quran,

> *Those who believed and those who suffered exile and strug-gled in the path of Allah — they have the hope of the Mercy of Allah. And Allah is Oft-forgiving, most Merciful.*[15]

This verse talks about those who can hope for the mercy of Allah, for they have done what was in their ability to win Allah's forgiveness.

Being over-confident in the mercy of Allah without making any effort is foolhardy. Allah describes in Surah Al-Aaraaf a people who were foolish and arrogant. They assumed that they were guaranteed their Lord's forgiveness, but did not take any steps towards Him.[16] Unlike such people, the hope that we aim for is one that is grounded in action.

15 The Quran, 2:218.
16 The Quran, 7:169.

A stronger sense of hope can be instilled through knowledge and action. Know the grace and gentleness of Allah with His servants. He provides us with uncountable blessings although we disobey him. He delays punishment in order to give us chances to repent. With all of the mercy He shows us in this life, will He really leave us to be destroyed forever in the Hereafter? The Prophetﷺ said, "By the One in whose hands is my soul, if you never committed sins, Allah would replace you with a people who sinned and repented so that He could forgive them."[17] The Prophetﷺ also said, "None of you should face death without expecting the best from Allah."[18]

This knowledge must be coupled with action, in order for the hope to be complete. You must be determined to improve yourself and take concrete steps to express the hope you have for the mercy of Allah. Hope must be accompanied by good actions, avoiding sins, and constant contemplation of both Allah's reward and punishment. This contemplation will teach the heart to love Allah and flee to Him. When a soul loves Allah, it must hope for His mercy and pleasure.

Balancing Fear and Hope

Is it better to have a heart filled more with fear? Should hope be predominant? Or should the two be equal? The answer to these questions depends on your natural disposition, as well as the state of your heart and your weaknesses.

If your heart feels overly secure, believing yourself to be beyond the punishment of Allah and guaranteed a place in Paradise, believing many of your blessings to be fruits of your own hard work, then it is better to work on restoring a stronger element of fear. On the other hand, if your heart is challenged with feelings of hopelessness and despair, and you think that the forgiveness of Allah will never

17 Muslim.
18 Muslim.

reach you, then it is better for you to concentrate on hope coupled with action. As for the one who is working on a high level of God-consciousness, seeking to leave all sins for the sake of Allah, then it is best to balance fear and hope equally. It was once said, "If the fear and hope of a believer were weighed, they would be equal."

Many of the companions skillfully balanced the two elements of hope and fear in their own hearts. Ali ibn Abi Talib said to some of his children, "My children, fear Allah to the extent that if you were to come to Him with the good deeds of the entire world, you would think that He might not forgive you. And have hope in Allah to the extent that if you were to come to Him with the bad deeds of the entire world, you would think that He might forgive you." Umar ibn Al-Khattab said, "If all of mankind were to enter the Fire except for one person, I would hope that person would be me. And if all of mankind were called to enter Paradise except for one, I would fear that one person would be me."

Thus, hope and fear complement each other, and must be balanced in the heart of a believer. If one overwhelms the heart, then that person is lacking an essential characteristic that could help him or her in the service of Allah. There are times when one may temporarily overshadow the other, but not permanently.

When one is near death, it is best for the heart to be flooded with hope. As in the hadith mentioned earlier, we should approach death expecting the best from Allah. When a heart is filled with hope, the soul will eagerly await its meeting with Allah. We know that whoever loves to meet Allah, Allah loves to meet him or her. If the heart instead is filled with fear, this may lead the person to dread meeting Allah because he has lost hope in the mercy and forgiveness of Allah. May Allah save us from such an end.

Reliance on Allah

{ *And if any one puts his trust in Allah, Allah is sufficient for him.* } [1]

In Arabic, tawakkul means to have complete reliance only on Allah, while taking all necessary measures and doing all actions to reach a goal. After all has been done, the heart relies totally on its Creator to bring about the results. A mutawakkil is a Muslim who practices tawakkul and puts his full trust in Allah. Prophet Muhammad ﷺ once said,

> If you were to trust in Allah to the utmost as He should be trusted, you would be provided for as the birds are provided for. They set forth in the morning hungry and return full and satisfied. [2]

Working to Bring About Something Does Not Contradict Tawakkul

Some may think that trusting in Allah means that we can just wait around for blessings and provision to fall from the sky—if something is meant to be, it will be. However, working and striving do

1 The Quran, 65:3.
2 Tirmidhi: hasan.

not contradict tawakkul. In fact, they are necessary for tawakkul to
be complete. Allah says in the Quran, ⟨It is He Who has made the
earth an accommodation for you, so traverse through its tracts and
enjoy of the Sustenance which He furnishes: but unto Him is the
Resurrection.⟩[3]

In the famous story, a man once asked the Prophet⟨ﷺ⟩ how he
should best safeguard his camel. "Should I tie it up and trust in Allah?
Or should I just leave it untied and trust in Allah to guard it for me?"
The Prophet answered, in what has become a timeless saying, "Tie
your camel, then trust in Allah."[4] Umar, may Allah be pleased with
him, said, "The one who relies on Allah sows his seeds first, then puts
his trust in Allah." Seeds will not sprout by themselves and produce a
full crop of food—we must work and tend the crop to reap the fruits,
while still putting our trust in Allah that only He can bring about the
final results. We know also, as in the first hadith, that even the birds
must fly and work to find their food, although it is guaranteed for
them by Allah!

No one should say that they practice tawakkul if they do not lift the
food to their lips to eat, instead waiting for Allah to deliver the food
to their mouths. Allah is certainly capable of making the food move or
giving a body the ability to survive without food, and yet the Creator
has set laws for His creation. One of those laws is that we are required
to work for our goals. We cannot expect to be instantaneously cured
of an illness unless we search for a cure and nurse ourselves back to
health. The Prophet⟨ﷺ⟩ said, "There is no illness except that Allah has
created a cure for it. Some will know the cure, and some will not."[5]

This law of cause and effect is one of many laws of creation that
Allah has established. Someone who applies himself and works hard

3 The Quran, 67:15.
4 Tirmidhi: hasan.
5 Bukhari and Muslim.

to achieve something will often achieve it. The one who does not work nor take any steps towards a goal will not achieve it.

It is certainly possible that someone works very hard to achieve something and does not reach their aim for reasons that only Allah knows. Perhaps they fell short of what was required, their faith is being tested, or they are being kept away from something that would be harmful to them. Allah has told us in the Quran that there may be things that happen to us that we do not like but that are good for us. Similarly, there may be things that make us very happy but are not good for us in the end.[6]

Once you have exhausted all of your options and strived all you can to reach a goal, you should have complete reliance on Allah. All of the worry and anxiety should disappear because He is in charge of your affairs. He is enough for you.

Prophet Muhammadﷺ took every possible step to ensure the success of the hijrah, the emigration to Madinah. Yet while he was in the cave and could see the feet of his enemies only inches away from him, there was nothing more that he could possibly do. He left the rest to Allah, completely at peace and trusting in His Lord to take care of him. And Allah helped him escape his enemies, even though they only had to look down at their feet to spot their target. Allah is not bound by the laws that He has created for us and may act outside of those laws from time to time as He wills in order to show us the greatness of His power.

Taking precautions does not contradict tawakkul
A Muslim must work to save, plan, and guarantee security in the future. The Prophetﷺ used to sell the crops of Banu Nadir and store a year's allowance for his family.[7] Prophet Muhammadﷺ said, "It is

6 The Quran, 2:216.
7 Bukhari.

better for you to leave your family well-provided for in case of your death than for you to leave them penniless, obliging others to care for them."[8] One must beware of allowing these precautions to lead to greed and amassing wealth, neither giving charity nor giving people their rights.

It is wrong to think that you can get closer to Allah by asking Him to give you trials and to test your faith, for you do not know if you will be patient through those difficulties. Rather, it is more appropriate to wish that Allah keeps hardships away from you and instead attempt to grow closer to Him by other means. Seeking to save yourself from falling into hardship, through every possible, righteous means, does not contradict tawakkul nor does it mean you are not content with the will of Allah. The Prophetﷺ ordered the Muslims of Makkah to migrate to Ethiopia during the early stages of Islam in order to protect them from harm and to safeguard the future of Islam.

The Prophetﷺ used to ask His Lord to give him health and wellbeing in his faith, this world, and the Hereafter. Umar ibn Al-Khattab forbade his armies from entering cities that had been infected by the plague. Someone asked him, "Are you fleeing from the will of Allah?" Umar answered, "I am fleeing from the will of Allah to the will of Allah." In this perceptive answer, Umar explained that he was escaping illness in favor of health, which was the will of Allah. Taking precautions is a necessary component of tawakkul and is one of the obligations of the Muslim.

---

8 Muslim.

Contentment

Conviction that Allah has created and preordained the entire universe, good and evil, is fundamental in the belief system of a Muslim. It is one of the six pillars of faith. Without this conviction, the Muslim's faith is incomplete.

Contentment and satisfaction with what Allah has ordained is a higher, more perfect degree of faith. Beyond merely believing in preordainment, the believer is content with whatever Allah gives her and plans for her. It is a sign of deep trust and love for Allah. Allah is pleased with the believer who is content with His will.

Allah says in the Quran, ⟨Allah is well pleased with them, and they with Him: all this for such who fear their Lord and Cherisher.⟩ The pleasure of Allah is greater than the bounties of Paradise itself—the greatest delight we will experience in Paradise will be winning the pleasure of Allah.[1] After that, there is nothing comparable. It is the key to every joy in Paradise. The Prophetﷺ said, "Allah will approach the believers in Paradise and tell them, 'Ask me for something.' The believers will respond, 'We want You to be pleased with us.'"[2]

1 The Quran, 9:72.
2 At-Tabarani.

Ali ibn Abi Talib once said,

> Whoever is content with what Allah ordained for him will have to endure it, all the while earning reward. Whoever is not content with what has happened to him will still have to endure it, but his deeds will be worth nothing.

Ibn Masud said,

> Allah in His justice and knowledge placed tranquility and happiness in the hearts of those who are confident and content in Allah's will. And He put anxiety and sorrow in the lives of those who are angry with the will of Allah.

The believer should be content with what Allah has willed, be it blessing or hardship. There are several reasons for this contentment, which your can remind yourself of when contentment is difficult.

The believer should know that Allah's planning is greater than her own. Allah reminds us in the Quran, ❴It is possible that you dislike a thing which is good for you, and that you love a thing which is bad for you. But Allah knows, and you know not.❵[3] The Muslim should also know that any difficulty is purification for her sins, if she is patient and obedient to Allah. Any difficulty can be a source of reward from Allah—if you have a contented state of mind. The Prophetﷺ said, "The believer, male or female, will continue to be tested in his or her self, children, and possessions, until he or she meets Allah without a single sin."[4]

A deep love for Allah will help the young Muslim to be contented with His will. This love embraces everything that comes from Allah the Almighty, even if it may be painful. This pain does not distract the believer from filling her heart with the love and adoration of Allah, for she knows without doubt that Allah's will is for the best. There

3 The Quran, 2:216.
4 Tirmidhi: hasan sahih.

are many examples of people who have suffered trials from Allah but whose hearts were still overflowing with love.

An example is a soldier who fights for the cause of Allah against injustice and tyranny. The Prophet ﷺ said about such a person, "When the believer is killed for the sake of Allah, his death hurts him no more than you would feel the bite of an ant."[5] This absence of pain is due to a heart overflowing with love, occupied only with hope of forgiveness and Paradise. Because the heart is so engaged, Allah relieves this Muslim of the pain sensation during death.

Contentment and Predestination

Contentment with the will of Allah does not mean being resigned to your own bad habits or sins. Nor does it mean that we have no control over whether we are guided or astray. Some people misunderstand the concept of being pleased with Allah's will; they think it is better to accept their sins and weaknesses, because such is contentment with Allah's will! This misperception will lead to downfall and indulgence in sin and is a trap of shaitan.

Allah ordained free will for every human being. He granted each one of us the ability to choose between guidance and darkness. The Quran reminds us that every soul is shown the path of good and evil and is given the freedom to choose without any restraint on that freedom. Allah knows what lies in our futures and knows—because He is beyond the constraints of our time dimension—what each one of us will choose. Allah already knows which one of us is of Paradise or of Hell, based on what we will choose for our own selves.

There is no contradiction in preordainment and our own free will. We should be convinced of this from the bottom of our hearts, for we know that Allah is the Just, the All-Knowing, the All-Merciful. He would never be unfair in the slightest, nor would He wrong a single

5 Tirmidhi.

being. If you are from the people of Paradise, then it is because you chose that for yourself. If you are from the people of sin and Hell-fire, then it is because of your own decisions—there is no one to blame but yourself for obeying the shaitan who whispered in your heart.

Is Making Supplication a Sign of Discontent with my Situation?
Making dua, supplication, that Allah gives you something or changes your circumstance does not contradict being content with Allah's will. Rather, it is something that we are commanded to do and a tool that we are given to change our situations. Allah commands us to call upon Him, ❨Call on your Lord with humility and in private.❩[6] The Prophetﷺ and the companions used to constantly make supplication, including supplications for relief from affliction. Just as thirst is relieved by drinking water, suffering is relieved by supplication. In fact, supplication is necessary in building contentment in the heart. It helps you to purify your heart, humble yourself before Allah, and entrust all of your affairs to Him.

6 The Quran, 7:55.

Refraining from Worldly Indulgence

Zuhd in Arabic means to expel from the heart any deep attachment to this world and instead focus on attaining what is better in the next life. Allah says, ❴What is with you will vanish, and what is with Allah will endure.❵[1]

Some people think that zuhd entails living in poverty, withdrawn from life and having very few worldly possessions. It would be irrational for that to be so, when the Prophetﷺ used to supplicate, "O Allah! Make the wealth and provisions of the people of Muhammad abundant."[2] The Prophetﷺ prayed for bounties for the Muslims, instead of encouraging them to remain in poverty and at the mercy of people.

This supplication was made assuming that the wealth of the Muslims would not make them preoccupied with the pleasures of this world, but rather make them strong and able to fulfill their mission. How many rich people, such as the two companions Uthman ibn Affan and AbdurRahman ibn Awf, did not allow their wealth to distract them from pursuing the Hereafter! And how many poor people were so consumed by their plight that it distracted them from the greater aim of their existence.

1 The Quran, 16:96.
2 Bukhari and Muslim.

The true meaning of zuhd is to carry the world and its bounties in the palm of your hand, and not in your heart. You employ what Allah has blessed you in obeying Him, serving others, and building a better world as Allah's vicegerent on earth. Beware of allowing the world to penetrate your heart and indulge only in what will energize the soul, rest the body, and help you to fulfill your responsibility. Allah says, ❨Seek, with the wealth that Allah has bestowed on you, the Home of the Hereafter, but do not forget your portion in this world.❩[3]

Avoid becoming so extreme in abstaining from worldly pleasures that you suffer burnout and lose resolve. The Prophetﷺ said, "The best of all is that which is balanced."[4] Once, the Prophet was told of three men who each imposed on themselves extreme restrictions—fasting excessively, praying constantly, and abstaining from marriage. The Prophetﷺ responded to this news by saying, "As for me, I fast sometimes and sometimes do not. I pray at night, but I also sleep. I marry women. Whoever strays from my example is not from me."[5]

Balance is the spirit of Islam. We were commanded to practice this spirit throughout our entire life: in our worship and daily affairs, in our eating and drinking, our sleep and movement, our spending and saving, our buying and selling, our solemn moods and our happiness, our dislikes and our desires, our speech and our silence. Our every decision and action should breathe moderation and balance.

---

3 The Quran, 28:77.
4 Al-Bayhaqi.
5 Bukhari and Muslim.

Loving Allah

A man asked the Messenger of Allahﷺ when The Hour would befall.

"And what have you prepared for it?" asked the Prophet.

"Messenger of Allah, I haven't prepared much in the way of extra fasting, prayers, or charity. But I love Allah and His messenger."

"You will be with those whom you love," responded the Prophetﷺ.[1] It is said that the happiness the companions felt when they heard this hadith was greater than any they had ever experienced, other than their happiness upon entering into Islam.

How can we love Allah? How do we instill that love in our hearts? Love of Allah is achieved through knowledge and action. The kind of knowledge that we need to increase our love for Him is a consciousness of His blessings and mercy upon us. It is in our nature to love the one who is kind to us, treats us well, and stands by our side in difficulty. It is also in our nature to love the one who has noble, beautiful, and perfect characteristics. Through learning about Allah and His attributes, as earnestly as we can, we will come to love Him. His attributes and His blessings extend beyond the reaches of our

1 Agreed upon.

imagination. Nurturing this knowledge and awareness will help us to love Allah.

There are so many practical actions we can take to increase our love for Allah; a few are mentioned here. Continuously contemplate the characteristics of Allah, His perfection, and His blessings on His servants. Draw closer to Allah through good actions and distance yourself from anything that displeases Him. We know that if we love someone, we will try as hard as we can to stay close to him and be with him whenever we can. That intimacy and closeness in turn increases the feelings of love and attachment. The closer we come to Allah and the more we do to please Him, the more our love for Him will grow.

Avoid whatever distracts you from Allah. We should be preoccupied with this life only to the extent necessary to give us the means and strength to reach the Hereafter in the best possible state. It is our nature that when we love someone, we want nothing else to come between us.

Signs that Allah Loves His Servant

In the famous hadith qudsi, Allah says,

> There is no better way for My slave to draw closer to Me than by doing what I have made obligatory upon him. My slave will continue to come closer to Me through extra actions until I love him. When I love My slave, I become the hearing with which he hears, the sight by which he sees, the hand he commands with, and the legs that carry him. If he asks Me, I will give him. And if he seeks refuge in Me, I will protect him.[2]

2 Bukhari.

This hadith lists many signs of Allah's love for a person. One of those signs is guidance, which is reflected in the heart, the mind, and the body in increased good deeds and acts of worship. Allah says in another famous hadith qudsi, "Whoever comes closer to Me by a hand's span, I come towards him an arm's length."

Another sign that Allah loves His servant is that He grants him ease in worldly affairs: "If he asks Me, I will give him. And if he seeks refuge in Me, I will protect him." Finally, a slave who is loved by Allah will be tested in both ease and hardship. The Prophetﷺ was asked, "Who are those most severely tested?" He answered,

> First the Prophets are tested the most, then the righteous people, then those who are of lesser faith. A man will be tested according to his faith. If he is firm on his religion, he will be tested more. If he is weaker, his tests will decrease. Difficulties will continue to befall the servant until he walks on the earth free of every last sin.[3]

Signs that a Muslim Loves His Lord

We must also scrutinize our own actions to see if our love for Allah is truly reflected in our behavior. The servant who loves Allah races to obey his Lord and to follow the example of His messenger. Allah says in the Quran, {Say: 'If you do love Allah, Follow me [the Prophet]. Allah will love you and forgive your sins—For Allah is Oft-Forgiving, Most Merciful.}[4]

If we love Allah, we will find ourselves constantly thinking of Him and remembering Him. Our thoughts are preoccupied with the people and things that we love. If our love for Allah is greater than our love for anything else, we should be remembering Him

3 Tirmidhi: hasan sahih.
4 The Quran, 3:31.

very often! Remembrance may be in the form of seeking forgiveness and praising Him, saying "La ilaha illa Allah,"[5] "Subhanallah,"[6]
"Alhamdulillah,"[7] "Allahu Akbar,"[8] and renewing intentions before
every action. Any action that is good and has pure intentions is a
way to remember Allah.

Love of Allah will also be manifested through a heart that is merciful towards all believers and stands up to those who oppress others
and hide the truth. Such a believer fears only Allah:

> ❴ *O Believers! If any from among you turn back from his Faith,*
> *soon will Allah produce a people whom He will love as they*
> *will love Him—humble among the believers, mighty among*
> *the disbelievers, fighting in the way of Allah and fearing not*
> *the blame of any defamer.* ❵ [9]

Love of Allah will also bring about contentment with whatever
Allah has given you. A Muslim filled with love for Allah will be in-
tensely eager to meet Him. He will sincerely hope and pray for that
Day to be one of joy and reunion with the Creator. It is only expected
that when we love something, we should look forward to coming face
to face with it. Such it is with our love for Allah.

5 "There is no God but Allah."
6 "Praise be to Allah."
7 "All Thanks is due to Allah."
8 "Allah is Most Great."
9 The Quran, 5:54.

God-consciousness

Taqwa can be roughly translated as God-consciousness. It encompasses not only awareness, but also a sense of awe and fear of Allah that leads one to obey Him. The muttaqeen are those who carry taqwa in their hearts and implement that awareness in all of their actions. These special individuals are described extensively in the Holy Quran.

Characteristics of the *Muttaqeen*
The beautiful, expansive nature of taqwa can be understood from the various ways in which Allah describes the muttaqeen in the Quran. Presented here is a collection of verses describing those who have God-consciousness and a brief analysis of what the verses tell us about this characteristic and those who are honored with it.

> ❨ *This is the Book; in it is guidance sure without doubt to the muttaqeen. Those who believe in the Unseen, are steadfast in prayer, and spend out of what We have provided for them; And who believe in the Revelation sent to you and that sent before your time, and in their hearts is surety of the Hereafter.* ❩ [1]

From these verses, we can see a description of the people who have God-conciousness. They believe in the unseen: in Allah, His angels,

1 The Quran, 2:1-4

His books, His prophets, the Day of Judgment, Paradise and Hell, and eternal life in the Hereafter. They observe prayer and spend their money in good causes. They follow and implement the commandments of the Quran in all of their affairs.

> ❦ *It is not righteousness that you turn your faces towards east or west; but it is righteousness to believe in Allah, the Last Day, the Angels, the Book, and the Messengers; to spend of your substance, out of love for Him: for your kin, the orphans, the needy, the wayfarer, for those who ask, and for the ransom of slaves; to be steadfast in prayer and practice regular charity; to fulfill the contracts which you have made; and to be firm and patient, in suffering and adversity, and throughout all periods of panic. Such are the people of truth, the muttaqeen.* ❧ [2]

In this verse, more characteristics of the muttaqeen can be discovered. We gather that a Muslim with taqwa is faithful to all of her promises: faithful to her promise to Allah by following His commands; faithful to the Messenger by following his example and supporting his cause; faithful to her own self by striving only for what is good. A Muslim with taqwa is also faithful to all Muslims and people of other faiths by keeping her word, keeping her appointments, fulfilling her contracts, and so on. A second characteristic mentioned in the preceding verse is patience and perseverance in all circumstances, in both prosperity and hardship.

> ❦ *Say: Shall I give you glad tidings of things far better? For those who have taqwa are Gardens in nearness to their Lord, with rivers flowing beneath. Therein is their eternal home, with pure companions and the good pleasure of Allah. For in Allah's sight, His servants are those who say, "Our Lord! We*

2 The Quran, 2:177.

have indeed believed. Forgive us our sins, and save us from the agony of the Fire;" They are those who show patience, firmness, and self-control; who are true in word and deed; who worship devoutly; who spend in the way of Allah; and who pray for forgiveness in the early hours of the morning.[3]

The muttaqeen frequently seek the forgiveness of Allah, especially in the hours before dawn, a special time for supplication. The Prophetﷺ said, "Our Lord descends to the lowest sky in the last third of the night and says, "Who is calling upon Me, that I may answer him? Who is asking of Me, that I may give him? Who is seeking My forgiveness, that I may forgive him?"[4] As the above verses indicate, the muttaqeen also possess the characteristic of humility and submission to Allah's will.

Be quick in the race for forgiveness from your Lord, and for a Garden whose width is that of the heavens and of the earth, prepared for the muttaqeen—those who spend freely, whether in prosperity, or in adversity; who restrain anger, and who pardon all men, for Allah loves those who do good. And those who, having done something to be ashamed of or wronged their own souls, earnestly bring Allah to mind and ask for forgiveness for their sins—and who can forgive sins except Allah?—and are never obstinate in persisting knowingly in the wrong they have done.[5]

In the past We granted to Moses and Aaron the criterion [to distinguish between good and evil], a Light and a Message for the muttaqeen. Those who fear their Lord in their most secret thoughts and who hold the Hour of Judgment in awe.[6]

3 The Quran, 3:15-17.
4 Bukhari.
5 The Quran, 3:133-135.
6 The Quran, 21:48-49.

In these two verses, the characteristics of the muttaqeen are described vividly. They spend from their wealth whether they are in a period of ease or financial strain. They control their temper and forgive easily. They are quick to seek forgiveness and return to Allah after they make mistakes. Those who have taqwa fear Allah not only outwardly, but more importantly in their deepest thoughts. They are in fervent anticipation of the Day of Judgment; those feelings translate into preparing for the Last Day with righteous deeds.

Taqwa: A Source of Honor

When taqwa resides in the heart of a human being, she does not need someone to be watching her in order to behave righteously. She is internally motivated by her awareness of Allah. Her taqwa becomes a vanguard that blocks out evil and facilitates the path to good. When the members of a community all possess this characteristic of taqwa, the society will bloom and flourish.

The Quran is replete with descriptions of how beloved the characteristic of taqwa is to Allah. When reading such descriptions, we should feel motivated to be among those who can enjoy such love, honor, and care from Allah. Our Lord designated taqwa as an indicator of how honored we are in His sight: ⟨Verily the most honored of you in the sight of Allah is he who is the one with the most taqwa.⟩[7]

Taqwa is the finest provision that we can equip ourselves with in this life, so seek to plant it in yourself: ⟨And take a provision with you for the journey, but the best of provisions is taqwa.⟩[8] Actions are accepted readily from those who have taqwa, ⟨Allah accepts the actions of the muttaqeen.⟩[9] Taqwa is a way out in difficult places, an escape route from stress and hardship, and a fountain of provision and ease: ⟨And for those who have taqwa, He ever prepares a way

7 The Quran, 49:13.
8 The Quran, 2:197.
9 The Quran, 5:27.

out, And He provides for him from sources he never could imagine. [...] and for those who have taqwa, He will make their path easy.}[10] Allah loves those who have taqwa, {Allah loves the muttaqeen}[11] and it brings about victory and a good end, {And the end is for the muttaqeen.}[12]

The Fruits of *Taqwa*

Taqwa has many positive manifestations in human character. Among them are trustworthiness, ihsan, modesty, and an unwavering sense of justice. These characteristics are described in more detail below, and come from a deep-rooted taqwa which makes the heart ever conscious of Allah.

1. *Trustworthiness.* Trustworthiness goes beyond just returning what is entrusted to you and fulfilling your promise. Those are certainly important aspects, but trustworthiness extends beyond the limited sense we commonly give it. Allah says in the Quran, {O you who believe! Betray not the trust of Allah and the Messenger, nor misappropriate knowingly things entrusted to you.}[13] The Prophet said, "There is no faith for the one who is not trustworthy. There is no religion for the one who does not keep his word."[14]

Trustworthiness is to fulfill a commitment or an obligation to your utmost ability. You expend the maximum effort, realizing that Allah is watching you and knows what you are ultimately capable of. The Prophet said,

> Each of you is a shepherd and each of you is accountable for his flock. A leader is responsible for the people who follow him. A man is a shepherd of his family and

10 The Quran, 65:2-4.
11 The Quran, 9:4.
12 The Quran, 7:128.
13 The Quran, 8:27.
14 Ahmad.

is responsible for them. A woman is a shepherd of her husband's home and is responsible for all therein. A servant is a shepherd of his master's possessions and is responsible for them.[15]

As explained in this hadith, trustworthiness is also to give whatever you have been entrusted with its full right and to deal with it in a responsible and honest manner.

If you are in a position of responsibility, an aspect of trustworthiness is to elect or appoint people only to positions suitable for them. Abu Dharr narrates, "I asked the Messenger of Allah to give me a position of responsibility. The Prophet clasped my shoulder and said, "Abu Dharr, you are weak. Responsibility is a trust, and on the Day of Judgment it will be a source of anguish and regret—except for those who gave it its right and fulfilled what was required of them."[16]

Trustworthiness is also to shun all forms of cheating. The Prophet said, "Whoever cheats is not of us."[17] Trustworthiness includes guarding secrets, keeping quiet about private gatherings and protecting people's privacy. The Prophet said, "If a man speaks to another, and turns his head [to see if anyone is listening], then consider the conversation a trust."[18] He said, "A gathering is a trust, except for three kinds of gatherings: one in which blood is shed, a promiscuous gathering, or one that involves taking people's wealth wrongly."[19] In these latter cases, when keeping the gathering secret would bring about harm, the content of the gathering may be exposed to protect people's lives, honor, or property.

A deeper aspect of trustworthiness is to protect, guard, and productively use all of the blessings that Allah gave you. Blessings such as your health, talents, wealth, your spouse, and your children are all

15 Bukhari.
16 Muslim.
17 Muslim.

18 Abu Dawud.
19 Ahmad.

trusts from Allah. You will be held accountable for them all on the Day of Judgment, so use them in the service of Allah in this life. Allah says in the Quran, ❴Then, on that Day, you will be questioned about the blessings you enjoyed.❵[20]

2. *Ihsan.* The second fruit of taqwa is ihsan, which means to perform anything to the absolute best of your ability and purely for Allah. Ihsan applies to our prayers, daily actions, responsibilities, and habits. Allah commanded us in the Quran to observe ihsan, ❴Practice ihsan, for Allah loves those who have ihsan.❵[21]

When Jibreel asked the Prophet about the meaning of ihsan, the Messengerﷺ responded, "It is to worship Allah as if you see Him, for if you do not see Him, He surely sees you." Here, the Prophet described ihsan in our relationship with Allah. Before every action, we should draw on this awareness that Allah knows the inner workings of our heart and sees our every move. This awareness will help us to achieve ihsan and perfect any action we do.

3. *Haya'.* Haya', modesty and wariness due to the presence of Allah, is another fruit of taqwa. The Prophetﷺ said, "Haya' can lead only to good."[22] Haya' makes the soul humble and modest in the presence of Allah, the One who created it and provided for it.

"Be in haya' of Allah, as is most deserving," said the Prophetﷺ to his companions.

"We do have haya' of Allah," they responded. The Prophet answered,

> Rather, the one who has deserving *haya'* of Allah should guard his mind and what it contains. Guard his stomach and what it consumes. He should remember death and its trials. Whoever wants the hereafter should cast aside the

20 The Quran, 102:8.
21 The Quran, 2:197.
22 Agreed upon.

glitter of this life. The one who does that has a deserving
haya' before Allah.[23]

Haya' also leads a Muslim to be conscious of his dealings with
people. He neither harms them nor hurts them in any way, neither
through actions nor attitude. This behavior is for the sake of Allah
and not to gain people's approval. The Prophet said, "Amongst
what survived from the teachings of the early prophets is this: 'If you
feel no haya', do as you wish."[24] Haya' can sometimes be misunderstood and interpreted as shyness or timidity. This is a mistaken conclusion for it may lead to holding back in speaking the truth and
doing what is right.

4. *Strong practice of justice.* Practicing justice, as a result of taqwa,
is to give all people their true right, whether family, children, neighbors, friends, co-workers, or people you meet on the street. This exercise of justice is a commandment from Allah and whoever neglects
it has sinned.[25] The reward for exercising justice is Paradise. The
Prophet said,

> Seven will be shaded by Allah on the Day when there is no
> shade but His. The seven types of people are a just leader;
> a youth who grew up obeying Allah; a man whose heart was
> attached indelibly to the mosque; two people who loved
> each other for the sake of Allah, meeting and parting in
> that state; a man who was invited to an unlawful relation-
> ship with a beautiful, influential woman and refused, say-
> ing, 'I fear Allah,'; one who gives secretly in charity so that
> his left hand hardly knows what the right hand has spent;
> and someone alone who remembered Allah in solitude, so
> his eyes overflowed with tears.[26]

23 Ahmad.
24 Bukhari.
25 The Quran, 4:58.
26 Bukhari.
27 The Quran, 20:113.

When rooted in people's hearts, the effects of justice are tremendous and go beyond just individual reward. When there is a prevailing understanding of justice, members of a community feel at peace, knowing that their rights, reputation, and property will not be trespassed upon. Loyalty to such a community of peace and tranquility increases, and all people are willing to defend it and contribute to it. It is said that a country that promotes justice, although it disbelieves in Allah, will last so long as that justice is maintained, and a country that oppresses, though it may be called a Muslim nation, will fail to prosper while the oppression continues. A community in which there is no sense of justice and a disregard for the rights of people will be overcome with fear and insecurity. There will be little allegiance to such a community and disorder will prevail. The resentment may be so great that it leads its members to harm each other.

How to Achieve Taqwa
Taqwa is achieved through knowledge and action. To gain knowledge that can help in achieving taqwa, it is important to:

1. Learn about the Greatness, Might, and Magnificence of Allah.

2. Remember the horrors and difficulties of the Day of Judgment.

3. Learn about the manifestations and benefits of taqwa, many of which have been described here.

There are many practical recommendations for building the presence of taqwa in the heart. Some of these recommendations are:

1. *Frequently recite the Quran,* contemplate its meanings, and act upon its counsel. Allah says in the Quran, ﴾Thus have We sent this down, an Arabic Qur'an, and explained therein in detail some of the warnings in order that they may have taqwa or that it may cause their remembrance of Him.﴿[27]

2. *Be steadfast upon the teachings* and manners of Islam. Allah says, ❴But to those who receive Guidance, He increases the light of Guidance, and bestows on them their taqwa❵[28] and ❴Those who strive in Our cause We will certainly guide them to our Paths: For verily Allah is with those who have taqwa.❵[29] Taqwa and guidance, as these verses tell us, come as a result of determined, individual effort. There may be a period of intense effort and patience before the effects of taqwa can be noticed.

3. *Increase acts of worship, especially fasting.* Fasting has a strong relationship with taqwa; each complements the other. Time and again in the Quran, whenever fasting is mentioned, taqwa is linked to it.[30]

Degrees of Taqwa

Some scholars believe that wara', or scrupulousness, is a higher degree of taqwa. Some say wara' is a heightened piety, fear, and awareness of Allah, and others say that it is just another name for taqwa. As you may have no doubt guessed, taqwa has degrees, of which wara' may be the highest. Some examples of the levels of taqwa are described briefly here.

The first level of taqwa is to leave everything that is clearly forbidden by Allah, without exerting oneself to avoid that which is doubtful. The second level is to leave all that is doubtful. A person with this second level of taqwa will avoid all that is unclear whether it is permitted or forbidden in Islam. The Prophetﷺ said, "Leave what is doubtful for what is not doubtful."[31]

The third degree of taqwa is to leave even that which is allowed out of fear that it may possibly lead to something disliked by Allah. The

28 The Quran, 47:17.
29 The Quran, 29:69.
30 The Quran, 2:21, 183.
31 Tirmidhi: sahih.

Prophet🌿 said, "The slave of Allah does not reach the level of the muttaqeen until he leaves what is permissible fearing that he may fall into what is prohibited."[32] The fourth and highest degree is to leave all that does not lead one to Allah. Such a person does no action unless it brings her closer to Allah. She uses the permissible comforts of this world to strengthen herself for worship and to remain healthy in order to serve Him.

---

32 As-Suyuti: sahih.

Holding Ourselves to Account

Muhasabah, in Arabic, is to measure and hold ourselves to account. Umar ibn Al-Khattab said,

> Hold yourself to account before you are judged. Weigh your actions before they are weighed against you. And prepare yourself for the ultimate trial: {That Day shall you be brought to Judgment: not an act of yours that you hide will be hidden.}[1]

A young Muslim who is striving to work for the Hereafter must always keep Umar's advice in mind. Remind yourself when you wake up every morning that the fabric of your life is time. Before you lies a new day. Consider it an allowance from Allah and an opportunity for good actions with sincere intentions. Do not let this chance pass you by, for you may regret it on the Day when regret is of no benefit.

Promise Allah every morning that you will use every joint and faculty of your body only for performing acts of obedience to Him. Examine yourself throughout the day—have you remained faithful to your promise? If you find that you have kept your promise, feel hopeful that you may be winning the pleasure of Allah and reward

1 The Quran, 69:18.

in the Hereafter. This hope and happiness should encourage you to increase in your good actions.

If you find yourself slipping and falling short of your promise, reawaken the resolve you felt earlier. All intentions need to be renewed periodically—your resolve to spend the day in Allah's service is no different. Take a few minutes from your day to refocus and remind yourself why you were created and how little time is left for you on earth.

Don't we know that death strikes suddenly?

Why can't we be patient for some fleeting moments so that we can enjoy eternal happiness with Allah?

If you find yourself ignoring your promise to Allah and going off in a completely different direction, you might find it helpful to impose a limitation on yourself. A productive penalty can be a useful tool in training yourself to have firm resolve and not be weak. Umar, may Allah be pleased with him, once missed a prayer in congregation. So he spent the entire night in prayer to make up for that missed opportunity.

The penalty you impose on yourself should be positive and should not be deprivation of physical necessities or painful in any way, physically or psychologically. Such self-imposed harm is a sin in itself, and will be punished even if it was intended to bring about increased worship. The purpose of this suggested measure is only to bring about renewed dedication to doing good.

Fulfilling the Rights of Others

The Rights Of Other Believers on You

Among the rights of every believer and every good, upright individual is that you do not harm them by speech or action. The Prophetﷺ said, "The Muslim is the one from whose tongue and hands other Muslims are safe from harm."[1] You must also protect the shortcomings and vulnerabilities of other Muslims. Sometimes, we may hasten to point out these weaknesses to every onlooker. Instead, we should shield our brothers and sisters from embarrassment and exposure, since the Prophetﷺ said, "Whoever covers another Muslim, Allah will cover his weaknesses in this life and in the Hereafter."[2]

Part of this shielding of your brother or sister is to refuse to listen to gossip and rumors about them, no matter how tempting. It goes without saying that we should not further the harm done by passing on those rumors and engaging in slander[3]: turning people against each other by spreading rumors. The Prophetﷺ said, "One who en-

---

1 Agreed upon.
2 Muslim.
3 See the chapter on slander.

gages in slander will not enter Paradise."[4] Slander propagates distrust
and hatred; it is said that if someone talks to you about another, be
sure that you have also been spoken about.

Another right that believers have upon you is for you to strive to
love them deeply and build your relationships with them. You should
love for your brothers and sisters what you love for yourself and wish
them to be free of whatever you dislike for yourself. Whenever you
are presented with an opportunity, be eager to serve them and help
them in every way. The Prophet said, "The believers, in their mutual love and mercy, are like a single body. If part of the body ails, the
entire body responds with fever and vigil."[5]

Advise your brothers and sisters when appropriate and with superior manners and discretion. The Prophet said to his companions,
"Help your brother whether he is the victim or oppressor."

"How do we help our brother if he oppresses?" asked the companions. The Prophet answered,

"Try to prevent him from oppressing."[6]

When two believers are fighting between themselves, their right
upon you is that you try your best to reconcile between them. A verse
in the Quran says, ❴Set aright matters of your difference.❵[7]

Among the rights of others upon you is that you respect those who
are older than you and show kindness to those who are younger. The
Prophet said that the one who does not show respect to the el-
der and mercy to the younger is not from his people.[8] Of course,
this mercy and kindness extends to all people of all faiths and backgrounds. The Prophet said that whoever does not show mercy to
people, Allah will not show mercy to him.[9]

4 Agreed upon.
5 Agreed upon.
6 Agreed upon.
7 The Quran, 8:1.
8 Abu Dawud: hasan.
9 Bukhari.

Our compassion and consideration should intensify when we deal with our parents, our children, our families, orphans, the sick, and the poor. Kindness to animals is also emphasized in Islam, and we will be held accountable if we mistreat the earth's creatures. The Prophetﷺ said, "A woman was sent to Hell because of a cat, which she tethered and starved, not even letting it free to catch its own food."[10]

We might think that our appearance is our own business, and that we look good in order to feel good. This is true to some extent—however, one of the rights our brothers and sisters have on us is that we keep ourselves clean, presentable, and smelling good! The Prophetﷺ said, "Five things should be performed to purify the body: shaving the pubic hair, circumcision, trimming the mustache, removing underarm hair and trimming the nails."[11] He also said, "Whoever has hair should take care of it."[12]

Following the example of the Prophet, you should be meticulous about your personal hygiene. Cleanse your mouth and freshen your breath before joining anyone's company or going to the mosque, using the best means available to you: "The siwak[13] purifies the mouth and pleases the Lord."[14] Putting on perfume is recommended for men. For women, it should not be a means of temptation and drawing men's attention to her presence—if a woman enjoys wearing perfume, it is better that she wears it in the privacy of her home or around family and other women.

Greeting other believers cheerfully and initiating the greeting to them is a social obligation and not a matter of personality or shyness. Sometimes we look the other way when we see someone pass by, or pretend not to notice them out of shyness. This was not the habit

10 Bukhari.
11 Bukhari.
12 Abu Dawud.
13 The siwak, a pleasant-smelling twig, was used
   for oral hygiene at the time of the Prophet.
14 An-Nisa'i.

of the Prophet☙ who always smiled in the face of his brothers and raced to be the first to greet them. He was always the last to withdraw his hand from a handshake. It is sunnah to shake hands, for the Prophet☙ said that when two believers meet and shake hands, they would be forgiven before they parted.[15]

A man, passing by the Prophet, said, "Assalam Alaikum."

"Ten rewards," the Prophet said. Another man came and greeted him, "Assalam alaikum wa rahmatullah."

"Twenty rewards," responded the Prophet. A third man walked by and said, "Assalam alaikum wa rahmatullah wa barakatuh."

"Thirty!" exclaimed the Prophet☙.[16]

It is also acceptable to kiss the hands of those people to whom you are indebted, such as your parents, the elderly, or people of great knowledge. Umar ibn Al-Khattab said that the companions used to kiss the hands of the Prophet, not out of obligation, but out of love and respect. Bowing out of respect is forbidden, because Muslims bow only to the Creator. Anas, may Allah be pleased with him, asked the Prophet, "When we meet one another, should we bow to each other?" "No," answered the Prophet. "Is it better that we kiss one another?" "No." "Should we shake hands?" "Yes."[17] In some narrations, it is said that the companions kissed one another in their greeting after an absence or travel.

Standing in admiration when someone enters a gathering is disliked in general; the one who does it will not be sinning, but the one who declines will be rewarded. The act becomes forbidden when it creates pride and self-admiration in the one who is shown the gesture. The Prophet☙ said, "Whoever feels pleased that people stand to greet him should take his seat in Hell."[18] However, standing up

15 Tirmidhi.
16 Tirmidhi.
17 Tirmidhi.
18 Tirmidhi: hasan.

when a deeply respected person enters, such as your parents or a just leader, is recommended because not doing so may be seen as disrespectful.

It is disliked to greet someone while in the bathroom. Once, the Prophetﷺ was greeted while he was relieving himself, so he did not answer.[19]

It is allowed for a man to greet a woman to whom he is not related, and vice versa. A group of men can also greet a group of women, and so on, as long as the greeting does not carry with it any flirtation or ill manners. Asma bint Yazid, may Allah be pleased with her, said, "The Prophetﷺ passed by us, a group of women, and greeted us."[20] If you suspect greeting someone from the opposite sex will open the door to temptation, then it is not allowed.

Another responsibility that we each have towards our brothers and sisters is to attend their funeral procession when they die. The Prophetﷺ said, "Whoever follows a funeral procession has one load of reward. Whoever remains until the end of the burial has two loads of reward."[21] This load is the size of Mount Uhud, according to another narration.[22] When we attend a brother's funeral, we remind ourselves of our own looming death and fulfill a right we owe to our fellow Muslim.

Visiting a brother or sister who is sick is another right that you must fulfill. The Prophetﷺ said, "If someone visits a sick person, he is engulfed in mercy. When he sits down, the mercy settles in him."[23] There is a detailed Islamic etiquette for visiting the sick. The Islamic prescriptions for visiting sick foster the remembrance of Allah, preserve the spiritual and physical wellbeing of the individual, and spread cordial feelings and brotherhood between people.

19 Muslim.
20 Tirmidhi: hasan.
21 Bukhari and Muslim.
22 Muslim.
23 Al-Hakim: sahih.

The etiquette for visiting the sick includes limiting the time spent in the presence of someone who is ill, sometimes only a few seconds if appropriate. This is so the ill person does not become exhausted or burdened by the visit. If the sick person wants the visitor to remain, and keeping him company would be beneficial to his spirits, then it is good to extend the visit. Discretion is favorable; refrain from asking probing questions about the illness and lower your gaze if the person is vulnerable or exposed. Instead, be gentle and make supplication for your sick brother, asking Allah to grant him an easy recovery.

If the sick Muslim's illness is contagious, then it is understandable that he should not be visited, or at least not touched or kissed if that is adequate to prevent infection. In several narrations, the Prophetﷺ ordered Muslims to avoid locations in which there was disease, because the health of a well person should not be risked for the sake of one who is sick. A quarantined sick person receives great reward for their patience in isolation and for protecting the health of their fellow Muslims. Indeed, as the Prophet explained, their reward is equivalent to that of the martyrs:

> A servant of Allah who is in a land afflicted with plague and must remain there without leaving [in order not to spread the disease], enduring patiently, knowing that nothing can afflict him except what Allah has written for him, will have reward such as that of a martyr for the sake of Allah.[24]

Another right that your Muslim brother and sister have upon you is that you respond with "Alhamdulillah"[25] after they sneeze. According to a hadith, the one who sneezed should say "Alhamdulillah," the one who responds should say, "Yarhamkumullah[26]," and the one who

---

24 Bukhari.
25 Thanks be to Allah.
26 May Allah have mercy on you.

sneezed should reply, "Yahdeekumullah wa yuslih balakum[27]."[28] If one sneezes while he is in the bathroom, he should say this silently.

Rights of Parents

"Prophet of Allah, who is the person most deserving of my companionship?" asked one of the companions.

"Your mother," responded the Prophet.

"And then who?"

"Your mother," the Prophet said again.

"And then?"

"Your mother. Then your father," said the Prophet.[29]

Another companion asked the Prophet, "O Messenger of Allah, is there anything I still should do to honor my parents after they have died?"

"Yes. Pray for them, seek forgiveness for them, fulfill any promises they made, honor their friends, and keep relations with their relatives," said the Messenger of Allah.[30] Most scholars rule that obeying our parents is a religious obligation, even in matters that are borderline or "gray areas" in Islam. However, it is not an obligation to obey them in matters that are clearly forbidden in Islam. For example, if you doubt that the food that your parents serve is lawful for you to eat, and you have tried your best to avoid the food yet they are deeply bothered, then you may eat what is necessary to please them — again, only if it is unclear whether the food is unlawful. This is because avoiding what is doubtful is a characteristic of taqwa, but obeying and gratifying parents is an obligation.

Similarly, if you wish to travel for a noble but voluntary cause in Islam, such as seeking knowledge abroad or participating in relief

27 May Allah guide you and put right your affairs.
28 Abu Dawud.
29 Muslim.
30 Al-Hakim: sahih.

efforts, but your parents do not wish you to, then you must obey them. However, if something is a religious obligation upon you, then you must perform the action despite their objections.

Children also have rights upon their parents, although it is not as emphasized in Islamic scholarship. This lack of emphasis is natural; parents naturally and intrinsically give their children their rights with more ease and love than children reciprocate as they grow older. Thus, Islam comes into play to balance the love and care of the parents with mutual respect, care, and attention from their children. However, some of the rights that children have upon their parents are described here for the benefit of young Muslims who are considering marriage or newlyweds, establishing new families and new homes.

A Muslim must provide for his children's material and emotional needs. A Muslim mother and father should be equally delighted whether they are blessed with a male or female child, for they do not know in which lies the most good. When the baby is born, the adhan[31] should be whispered in the ear of the newborn. The first sound the baby hears is the remembrance of Allah, as he or she begins a life that will be filled insha'allah with worship and blessings. Similarly, it is recommended that the first words the baby learns to speak are "La ilaha illa Allah."[32]

A Muslim mother and father should choose beautiful, decent names for their children. The Prophet⬥ said, "You will be called on the Day of Judgment by your own names and the names of your fathers. So choose your names well."[33] Another duty to perform for your children is the aqiqah,[34] if the newly blessed couple is financially

31 The call to prayer.
32 There is no God but Allah.
33 Abu Dawud.
34 A celebratory occasion upon the birth of a baby in which a sheep or goat is sacrificed and its meat served amongst the people.

capable of it. In this sunnah, the parents sacrifice either a goat or a sheep, one for a girl and two for a boy. One or two is recommended for a boy; it is narrated that the Prophetﷺ sacrificed only one sheep after the birth of his grandson, Al-Hasan. The aqiqah brings with it the reward of spreading happiness among the Muslims; not only are the new parents delighted themselves, but they spread their joy to others by gathering the community and sharing their food.

A Muslim mother and father must strive to raise their children according to the teachings and manners of Islam. Allah says in the Quran, ﴿O You who believe! Save yourselves and your families from a Fire whose fuel is men and stones...﴾[35] The scholars have interpreted "saving your families" to mean teaching them and raising them well. Another right that parents must fulfill towards their children is helping them as much as they can to get married when they are ready to do so.

Rights of the Spouse

The Muslim woman has rights over her husband, just as her husband has rights upon her. Fulfilling the rights of your spouse is a way to secure happiness and peace in your home, as well as the path to pleasing Allah and thanking Him for blessing you with a righteous partner. We will begin with the rights that a man owes to his wife.

1. *That he deal with her with the best character and manners.* Allah says, ﴿Live with [your wives] on a footing of kindness and equity.﴾[36] The kindness and good treatment that a wife deserves from her husband is not limited merely to him refraining from harm and insult; it also includes forbearance of her character faults and mistakes. The best example of this kind and just dealing was Prophet Muhammadﷺ. His wives would argue with him and sometimes refuse to talk to him for

35 At-Tahrim, 6.
36 The Quran, 4:19.

a day and night. The Prophet bore this with understanding, humility, and kindness.

2. *He should be a gentle, good-humored companion to her.* The Prophet said, "The believers with the most complete faith are those with the best character and the gentlest among their families."[37] He also said, "The best of you are those who are best to their women. And I am the best among you to my women."[38] However, the good-humored and playful atmosphere in the household should not reach the point of ridicule or flippancy between husband and wife.

3. He should spend with moderation upon the household. The husband should provide his wife with what she needs, being neither stingy with his money nor extravagant. Allah says, ⟨Eat and drink and do not be extravagant.⟩[39]

4. *He should be protective and covetous of his wife and family*, within moderation. A husband and father should hate to see his wife or daughter exposed to any humiliation or dishonor. This protectiveness should lead him to guard the honor of his family and encourage the female members of his family to conduct themselves according to Islamic teachings. However, this should not be so extreme that he becomes suspicious of his family members, questioning their every move. The Prophet said, "There is a type of jealousy which is hateful to Allah: that which leads a man to doubt his family members without any proof."[40]

5. *The husband and wife should observe Islamic etiquette during intercourse.* The couple should say "Bismillah"[41] before intercourse. The Prophet said,

37 An-Nisa'i.
38 Tirmidhi: hasan.
39 The Quran, 7:31.
40 An-Nisa'i.
41 In the name of Allah.

When one of you approaches his wife [for intercourse] and says, "In the name of Allah; O Allah keep shaitan away from us and away from any offspring You may bless us with," the shaitan will not be able to harm any child they are blessed with.[42]

They should also be sure that they are in complete privacy and that no one can see them. Seeking privacy during these moments is closest to the pure, natural tendencies that Allah instilled in each of us, and it increases the enjoyment of this pleasure that Islam made permissible for us.

The husband should approach his wife kindly and gently, talking to her and kissing her. He should also be mindful that she has the chance to satisfy her desire as well. He should make himself available to her when she needs him, at least every four nights. The couple can either increase or decrease the frequency, depending on their mutual needs. While she is menstruating, the husband should not have actual intercourse with her, although they can still enjoy intimacy and sexual satisfaction during that period.

6. *If a husband has more than one wife,* then their rights on him include that he deals with them equitably. He should provide for each wife a home of her own and be fair in spending equally on each of them. As for the one he feels the most love towards—that is a human feeling that is not under his control. Allah says in the Quran, ⟨You will never be able to be fair and just between women, however much you wish to do so.⟩[43] This verse refers to the inner feelings of the heart; just, equal treatment of more than one wife is an obligation.

7. *Rights during divorce.* Even during divorce, there are rights that a husband must fulfill towards his wife. A man should know that divorce is permissible in Islam, but Allah dislikes it most of all things

42 Agreed upon.
43 The Quran, 4:129.

that are permissible. It is a sin to harm, insult, demean, or harass the woman whom he is divorcing.

Divorce should not be a sudden decision that the husband executes at will. Rather, it is only a last resort after a series of prescribed attempts at reconciliation. When his wife violates the marital relationship and makes it impossible to live peacefully, the avenues available to a man are the following, in order: He should communicate with his wife, advise her, and counsel her many, many times before he moves to the next step. Then, he may warn her and caution her numerous times. The next step, after much effort, is that he may refuse to sleep at her side. He may leave the house for up to three nights, expressing his anger. If all of that has not worked, after many repeated attempts, he is allowed in Islam to chastize her, a light stroke that is symbolic and incurs no physical pain.

> *As to those women on whose part you fear disloyalty and ill-conduct, admonish them first, Next refuse to share their beds, And last hit them [gently]; but if they return to obedience, seek not against them means of annoyance: For Allah is Most High, great above you all.* [44]

If a husband and wife feel they will separate from each other after these measures, they should first elect two representatives from each of their families to act as arbiters in the conflict, as is detailed in a verse in the Quran. If they truly hope for reconciliation and do not wish to be parted, Allah will find a solution for them.[45]

A wife has rights upon her husband even as he is divorcing her, if there is no other solution than that. He should not divorce her when she is menstruating and he should not pronounce the divorce more than once, in case he decides to rescind. He should be extremely

44 The Quran, 4:34.
45 The Quran, 4:35.

careful not to disclose any of her secrets after the divorce. Finally, he should find it in himself to bestow a gift upon her, in compensation for the pain he caused during the divorce.

All of the stated obligations apply to the wife as well. There are also some specific rights which a wife must fulfill towards her husband. While many of the rights of a husband and wife overlap, a few characteristic ones specific to the woman are mentioned here.

It is a wife's duty to obey her husband as long as he asks her to do something that is not sinful. The reward the woman receives for this obedience is immense; the Prophetﷺ said, "If a woman prays her five prayers, fasts her month [of Ramadan], guards her chastity, and obeys her husband, she will enter her Lord's Paradise."[46]

A wife should seek to make her husband pleased whenever she can. She should not betray him nor deal irresponsibly with his property. She should be content with what wealth and provision he has been blessed with and not suspect that there is more that he is not giving her.

Among the rights of a husband upon his wife is that she raises his children with the best morals and principles. She should not leave the house if she does not have his permission to do so. If she is blessed with a righteous, kind husband who treats her nobly, she should realize the great treasure that she has. The Prophetﷺ said, "If I were to order anyone to prostrate to another, I would have ordered a wife to prostrate to her husband due to the gravity of the right he has upon her."[47]

Rights of Your Relatives

If you have any doubt about the importance of this principle of keeping relations with even your distant relatives, ponder the following ahadith. The Prophetﷺ said, "Whoever would like to increase his

46 Ibn Habban.
47 Tirmidhi.

lifespan and be granted expanse in his wealth should keep relations [with his family, relatives, and distant relations]."[48] He also said, "Keeping relations hangs from the throne of Allah. The one who will reach it is not the one who only keeps relations with those who welcome and accept him. Rather, the one who will reach it is the one who keeps relations with those who cut him off and avoid him."[49] And finally, "What is given to a poor person counts as charity. Wealth given to a relative counts as double: charity and keeping relations."[50]

Asma, the daughter of Abu Bakr, once asked the Prophet, "My mother has come to visit me, but she is a disbeliever. Should I keep my relations with her?" The Prophet responded, "Yes."[51] The principle of respect and honoring relations extends to all relatives, regardless of their faith or background.

The Rights of Your Neighbors

"Jibreel persisted in urging good treatment of neighbors until I expected him to say that our neighbors should be included in our wills,"[52] The Prophet said. He also said, "Some of the happiness of a Muslim can be found in a spacious home, a righteous neighbor, and a reliable means of transportation."[53]

Once the Prophet was asked about a woman who used to fast during the days and pray during the night, but was rude to her neighbor.

"She is in Hell-fire," said the Prophet.[54]

Among the rights that your neighbor has upon you is that you be the first to greet him or her. You should refrain from bothering your neighbors in any way, and if they bother you, bear the inconvenience patiently. You must visit your neighbor when she is sick, comfort her

---

48 Agreed upon.
49 Tabarani, & Bukhari with a
   different wording.
50 Tirmidhi, hasan.
51 Agreed upon.

52 Agreed upon.
53 Al-Hakim, sahih.
54 Al-Hakim, sahih.

in a calamity, and congratulate her on special occasions. You should lower your gaze from her home, refrain from peering into her windows while passing by, and not pry into anything that she might wish to remain secret.

If your neighbor is traveling, you should check on his family and help them if they need anything. You should also help your neighbor with any skills that he may require of you, as well as any counsel that he may benefit from in matters of this world or the Hereafter. All of these rights are in addition to the rights of any Muslim, which were mentioned in the beginning of this chapter.

The Right of Brotherhood in Islam

We have already discussed the rights of any Muslim upon another Muslim brother or sister. However, due to our human nature, we naturally long to have a special brotherhood or sisterhood with people whom we love or admire very much. This love, if it is for the sake of Allah, is the source of great reward and honor in the sight of Allah. However, it is also a relationship that demands extra commitment from us.

Brothers or sisters for the sake of Allah will inevitably have a great deal of influence on each other, for good or evil. Thus, when they are in each other's company, they should strive to let that influence be a source of reward and increased righteousness. They should work to make the time they spend together free of sin and filled with the remembrance of Allah. The Prophetﷺ said,

> The righteous companion is like a perfume seller. If he does not give you any of his goods, at least you will come away smelling beautiful. The bad companion is like a blacksmith. If you are not burned or dirtied in his company, you will at least come away smelling of fumes.[55]

55 Abu Dawud.

Brotherhood and sisterhood have worldly benefits as well. Your brothers and sisters in Islam support you and fortify you in the journey through this life. As it is said, we are one by ourselves, many with our brothers. The Prophetﷺ said, "One believer to another is like a brick wall. Each brick supports and upholds the other."[56] The value of a truthful, sincere brotherhood is immeasurable; you will see it in the tranquility it brings to your heart and the security it brings to your worldly circumstances. However, as we mentioned, this relationship has extra rights that must be fulfilled. Like a marriage, brotherhood or sisterhood is a serious commitment with serious obligations.

In addition to the rights you must fulfill towards any Muslim (see earlier section), your brother has a number of additional rights upon you. They include the following:

1. *Rights upon your wealth.* Ali ibn Al-Hussain, may Allah be pleased with him, once asked a man, "Do you ever put your hand into your brother's pocket or money bag and take what you need without asking?"

The man answered, "No!"

"Then you are not true brothers," Ali answered. There should be no ceremony or formalities between two brothers—they should be able to take from each other what they need without embarrassment. Some of the companions in Madinah gave their house keys to their brothers so they could take whatever they needed without permission. This was how deep the trust and care between them.

A Muslim's right upon his brother's wealth is of degrees. The least degree of which one cannot go below is to help your brother in financial difficulty before he is obliged to ask you for help. If he must humble himself to solicit your help, you have fallen short of fulfilling your brother's right upon you. The second degree is to share freely of your wealth with your brother, to the point that if he asked you

56 Bukhari.

to split it with him you would readily do so. The third and highest degree is to prefer your brother over yourself in your wealth and to think of his needs before your own.

2. *Rights upon yourself.* Among your brothers' or sisters' rights upon you are rights upon your own being: your thoughts, attention, and concern. You can fulfill this right by seeking to satisfy the material and emotional needs of your sister, which is also of degrees. The lowest degree is to respond when your sister requests a favor of you. The next degree is to be there before she has to ask you, sensing her need and fulfilling it before she has to verbalize it. The highest degree, preferring your sister over yourself, is to put her needs before your own.

One of your sister's rights upon you is that your heart be always free of any resentment, envy, or ill feelings toward her. The Prophet☽ said,

> Every Monday and Thursday, actions are presented to Allah. Allah will forgive on those days all who do not associate partners with Him, except for the one who harbors ill feelings towards his brother. For those two, Allah will say, "Leave them until they settle what is between them."[57]

3. *Rights upon your speech.* Your sister has a right upon your speech: that you do not backbite, spread rumors about her, expose her secrets, draw attention to her faults, or ridicule her. In other words, nothing that you say or listen to should be harmful or hurtful to her.

The only circumstance in which you may need to say something that would displease your sister is when you are speaking up for something good or preventing something evil. In such a case, when you cannot find any excuse to remain silent, you may speak in a kind manner that will encourage both of you to obey Allah.

57 Muslim.

Know that every human being has his strengths and weaknesses. We should select those people whose good surpasses their bad characteristics to be our close companions and brothers. Yet even they have shortcomings and will make mistakes. When we notice their weak points, we should not emphasize them in our own minds and instead should remember their good characteristics. Always call to mind the good in your brother so that the relationship between you remains strong. It is only the hypocrite who will meticulously pick out the faults in another—be sure to remain occupied with your own faults rather than the faults of your brother.

Another right upon your speech is that you say the things that will make your brother happy, such as calling him by a nickname that he likes, asking frequently about him, defending him when people talk about him, and communicating with him about the brotherhood and love between you. This should be done in the proper Islamic manner, without falling into flattery, lying, remaining silent while your brother is in the wrong, or refraining from giving advice in order not to offend him.

4. *Forgiving his shortcomings and mistakes.* It is likely that at some point, your brother will fall short in his relationship with you; either by having some shortcoming that affects his faith or by violating one of your rights on him.

If it is the first case, and your brother has fallen short of his religious obligations or committed some sin, then you must remain kind to him, advise him in privacy, and help him to improve himself and return to his former path of obedience. If he is insistent upon remaining as he is, do not break relations with your brother. Perhaps your friend is stubborn this time, but next time he will heed your words. The Prophetﷺ said, "It is not allowed for a Muslim to cut off his brother for more than three days."[58]

58 Bukhari.

Three days is the maximum length of time you may cut off contact; beyond that, the disregard is a sin. By ignoring or cutting off your brother, both of you are harming yourselves and the Muslim community is weakened one more degree. The best of you in the sight of Allah, and the one who will reap the greatest reward, is the one who extends the first greeting, forgives his brother even if he did not admit to his wrong, and deals with him as if the altercation never happened. The only circumstance in which a person is to be shunned is when he is openly lewd and corrupt, inviting others to evil without shame. If such corruption exists in a person but he hides it, then that is no reason to shun him. Rather, he should be approached gently and patiently counseled.

If your brother has wronged you personally and fallen short of his obligations towards you, then you may advise him privately. After that, the obligation is upon you to forgive him and tolerate his behavior if it continues. If he apologizes, then you should accept his excuses without question. If your brother didn't call on you during sickness or if he wasn't there for you when you needed him most, it is acceptable to let him know that you were upset or hurt, but in no way allow a rift to grow between you. If you continue to hold a grudge and doubt his excuses, then you will be blamed in front of Allah. Instead, race to forgive him and overlook his faults. The Prophetﷺ said, "Whoever receives an apology from his brother and does not accept it, he will accumulate sins like those of a corrupted tax-collector."[59]

5. *Loyalty and Sincerity.* This loyalty towards your brother or sister is a love that endures throughout life. After death, this loyalty continues by looking out for his or her children, family, and friends. The Prophetﷺ exhibited this loyalty towards his wife Khadijah long after she had passed away, by extending kindness to her old friends, visiting with them, and looking after their needs. [60]

59 Ibn Majah.
60 Al-Hakim, Sahih.

How to Increase Brotherhood

There are many things that brothers and sisters for the sake of Allah can practice to deepen the love and loyalty between them. Some of these practical measures are suggested here.

Brothers should get to know each other on a deep level, and should take opportunities to increase the friendship between them. The Prophet said, "If one of you has become a brother to another, you should ask him about his family, his lineage, and where he is from. It will help love to enter your hearts."[61]

When you love your brother and sister for the sake of Allah, say so! Tell them that you love them for Allah's sake, for as the Prophet indicated it brings the hearts closer and increases the love between them. Once, a man was sitting with the Prophet and someone passed by. The man turned to the Prophet and said, "Messenger of Allah, I love him for the sake of Allah."

"Have you told him so?" asked the Prophet.

"No."

"Then let him know," said the Prophet. This man went promptly to his brother in Islam.

"I love you for the sake of Allah," he said.

"May the one for Whom you love me, love you," responded the second man.[62]

Frequently visit your brother and sister in Islam. The Prophet said that whoever visits someone who is ill or visits a brother whom he loves for the sake of Allah, a voice calls from the sky, "You have performed goodness, your footsteps were blessed, and you have risen to a higher rank in Paradise."[63] Give gifts to your brother, for the

---

61 Tirmidhi.
62 Abu Dawud.
63 Abu Dawud.

Prophet also said that giving gifts increases love between people.[64] Avoid being burdensome to your brother. There are many popular sayings that warn against imposing too much on a friend, for that can ruin a relationship.

Finally, one of the most powerful tools in increasing brotherhood between you is to pray for one another. Make supplication for your sister in everything that you would want for yourself, because when you supplicate for your sister it is as if you are also supplicating for yourself at the same time. The Prophet☀ said, "If a man secretly supplicates for his brother, an angel will say, 'And may you have the same.'"[65] The Prophet also said in another hadith that the supplication for a brother in Islam without the other's knowledge will be accepted. Imagine that you make a supplication for your sister and she does not know of it. At the same time, she is supplicating for you without your knowledge. What a special, blessed relationship! Insha'allah, glad tidings await both of you.

Rights of the Teacher
Ali ibn Abi Talib detailed the rights of a teacher upon the student. These manners and obligations can be observed in the presence of anyone who has taught you something, be it something new about your religion, formal instruction, or a life lesson.

A student should not ask too many questions nor be picky and rude in accepting answers. If the teacher is forgetful or falls short of his responsibilities, do not nag him to the point of annoyance. Do not speak about your teacher with other students nor spread his secrets. Do not pounce on his errors nor look out for his mistakes; instead, when a teacher makes a mistake, excuse it and accept his apology

---

64 "Give gifts, and you will increase in love." Authenticated by Abu Ya'la.
65 Muslim.

without further thought. Do not always confront your teacher with, "Well, I heard so and so say differently…" Respect your teacher deeply, for the sake of Allah. Serve him in any of his needs or chores.

These manners are part of the Islamic reverence for knowledge and those who pursue knowledge. Islam honors those who walk the path of knowledge and gives them high status in this life and the Hereafter. Allah says, ﴾Are those equal, those who know and those who do not know?﴿[66] The Prophet said, "One scholar is a greater challenge to the shaitan than one thousand worshippers."[67]

Islam, its rulings, and systems are not a written list of rituals that are passed down to each generation. Instead, Islam requires each generation to produce great minds that can understand its principles and apply them. Our respect for teachers and scholars should extend from our reverence for knowledge and deep understanding. It is at their hands, with the help of Allah, that our religion is transmitted, preserved, and renewed.

66 The Quran, 39:9.
67 Tirmidhi.

Part III
Implementing Worship

Allah prescribed upon us acts of worship that are designed to empower our faith, shape our character, and better our individual and collective human condition. Worship in Islam is not merely rituals; rather, it is an expression of our obedience and submission to the Creator. It is also an invaluable tool of self-purification and personal development, as indicated in the Quran.

Every form of worship that we perform should leave an impression on our souls. Every form of worship instills a principle, rejuvenates our heart, and brings us one step closer to our Creator. Our hearts should find themselves recharged for action. Through this blend of worship, character, action, and self-revitalization, the Muslim personality is complete.

This personality that we are seeking to instill is sincere, earnest, and balanced. We hope to become someone who thinks, contemplates, develops, and improves; one who serves others, exercises patience in all circumstances, and is highly aware and mindful of Allah. When a Muslim who strives for these characteristics is joined by his brothers and sisters, this will lead to a flourishing, upright community that is capable of leading the world to a better place. This is our vision and purpose on earth; to be vicegerents of Allah, that we may win His pleasure and Paradise.

Personal development, of which implementing worship is a key step, is essential to enabling Muslim youth to take on this responsibility. By helping each individual achieve the vision of our faith in himself and translate it into action, we can actualize the mission of Islam among youth in America.

Prayer

Prayer is one of the most powerful tools of self-reformation. It is the link between you and your Creator. By engaging in prayer, you strengthen the principles of submission, oneness of God, and gratitude in your mind and heart. It is a shield against what is sinful and prohibited: ❴Surely prayer keeps one away from indecency and evil.❵[1] In order for prayer to give you the fruits of self-purification, it must be performed with awe and concentration.

During prayer, we strive for a presence of heart and mind. Our hearts should be overwhelmed by the greatness of Allah, His might, and His generosity. Our hearts realize how weak we are and how we have fallen short of worshiping its Creator. In prayer, the mind must also be present, contemplating the various actions of prayer. When the call to prayer is heard, the Muslim remembers the terror and regret many will feel when they are called to judgment on the Last Day.

During wudu[2], remember that outward purity should be paralleled by an inward purity, free from worldly attachment, self-love, arrogance, envy, and resentment. Upon standing in prayer, visualize what

---

1 The Quran, 29:45.
2 The ablution before prayer, also an act of worship.

it might be like to stand before Allah. Upon saying 'Allahu akbar', truly internalize that meaning: Allah is Greater than anything.

When reading Quran in your prayer, contemplate the meanings of the verses so that you are motivated to act upon them. During the different positions in prayer and during your praises, thanks, and supplication, think about the greatness, mercy and power of your Creator. When joining a congregational prayer, notice how no movement occurs without the leader and how all move in unison. Contemplate the collective spirit of the Muslims, their strength, discipline, and organization when they abide by their religion.

There are several practical steps you can take to help instill this presence of heart and mind in prayer. Some of them are recommended here:

1. *Clear your mind.* Take a few moments to dismiss the thoughts that clutter your mind before prayer. Upon hearing the call to prayer, focus on preparing yourself for the appointment that lies before you. You are about to meet your Creator.

2. *Utilize the time between the two calls to prayer.* The minutes between the adhan and iqamah[3] are a special window of time in which supplication is answered and in which the mind should be prepared for prayer. Remember Allah, seek His forgiveness, and read Quran during this time. It is recommended to remain quietly in the mosque before prayer, instead of talking or passing time elsewhere.

3. *During prayer, stay focused.* Keep your eyes riveted to the place where your forehead will touch the ground in prostration. Do not allow your sight to wander and hence your mind to become preoccupied. Contemplate every position you take during prayer, as described previously. Remember the hadith of the Prophetﷺ,

---

3 A second call to prayer immediately before the prayer starts.

Any Muslim who performs an obligatory prayer, perfecting his *wudu,* concentration, and prostrations, will have that prayer be a purification for all of his previous sins, except for major ones, and that is throughout his entire life.[4]

---

4 Muslim.

Fasting

The easiest way for the shaitan to ensnare the human soul is through the trap of desire and temptations. If you can resist temptation and control your desires, you have succeeded in blocking shaitan's manipulation. One of the best ways to increase your self-control and endurance against this assault is fasting.

If you can be patient in abstaining from that which is allowed in Islam: eating, drinking, and marital relations, then it should become easier to resist what is forbidden. The Prophetﷺ said, "Fasting is half of patience."[1] Fasting also leads directly to taqwa—an active consciousness of the presence of Allah and reverence of Him. Allah says in the Quran, ﴾Fasting is prescribed for you as it was prescribed for those before you, that you may attain taqwa.﴿

Degrees of Fasting

1. *General fasting.* General fasting is abstaining from food, drink, and marital relations. Many Muslims only observe this general type, without raising their aspirations to higher degrees. The Prophetﷺ said, "So many people achieve only hunger and thirst from their fasting!"[2]

1 Tirmidhi: hasan.
2 An-Nisa'i.

2. *Special fasting.* This second rank of fasting is to keep away from all sins, shielding the senses and body from any disobedience or evil. Hearing, sight, speech, hands, and feet all stay away from evil and are engaged only in goodness. This is the fasting of the righteous people. The Prophet☾ said,

> Fasting is a shield. If one of you is fasting, he should not commit obscenities nor should he behave foolishly. If he is confronted or insulted, he should respond, "I am fasting. I am fasting."[3]

3. *Extra-special fasting.* The third degree of fasting is to free the heart from preoccupation with this life. All awareness and motivation is directed towards Allah. This is the fasting of those who are very close to Allah.

Recommended Occasions for Fasting

Fasting during the month of Ramadan is obligatory on every capable Muslim. In addition to the obligatory fasts, there are many occasions on which it is recommended to fast. The one who does so will be rewarded, and the one who does not fast on those occasions will not be at fault. Some of the recommended occasions for fasting are mentioned here:

1. *Fasting Mondays and Thursdays.* Abu Hurayrah narrated that the Prophet☾ used to fast frequently on Mondays and Thursdays. When he was asked about this habit, he responded,

> Our deeds are presented to Allah every Monday and Thursday, and He forgives all believers, except for those who have hard feelings between them. For those, Allah will say, "For them, wait."[4]

3 Bukhari & Muslim.
4 Ahmad: sahih.

The Messengerﷺ loved to have his deeds presented on a day that he was fasting, so that Allah would bestow even more mercy upon him.

2. *Fasting three days of every month.* These three days are the 13th, 14th, and 15th day in every month of the Islamic calendar. Abu Dharr said, "The Prophet advised us to fast three days of every month: the 13th, 14th and 15th. He told us, 'It is like fasting for all of time.'"[5]

3. *Fasting the days of Arafah and Ashura.*[6] The Prophetﷺ said, "Fasting the day of Arafah erases the sins of two years, the previous and upcoming, and fasting the day of Ashura erases the sins of the past two years."[7]

4. *Fasting six days of Shawwal,* whether consecutively or not. The Prophet said, "Fasting the month of Ramadan and following it with six days of Shawwal is as if one fasted for all time."[8]

5. *During other Months.* It is also recommended to fast frequently during the months of Dhul-Qi'dah, Dhul-Hijjah, Muharram, Rajab, and Sha'ban. It is narrated by Aishah that the Prophet used to fast many days in Sha'ban.[9]

As for the young Muslim who has the strength and willingness to fast as much as he can, the most beloved fast to Allah is the fast of Prophet Dawud, which was to fast every other day, according to the hadith of Prophet Muhammadﷺ.[10]

---

5 Ibn Habban: sahih.
6 The 9th of Dhul Hijjah and the 10th of Muharram, respectively.
7 Muslim, An-Nisai, Ahmad & others.
8 Muslim, Tirmidhi, & others.
9 Agreed upon.
10 Ahmad & others.

Spending in the Cause of Allah

❴ Who is he that will loan to Allah a beautiful loan, which Allah will double in his credit and multiply many times?❵ [1]

The human self has an intrinsic element of greed and possessiveness which is described in the Quran.[2] Spending for the sake of Allah is the essential counterpart and a key step in purifying the soul. In the Quran, Allah says, ❴But those most devoted to Allah shall be removed far from [the Fire]—those who spend their wealth for increase in self-purification.❵[3]

In order for spending to have an effect on the soul, several elements must be present. A pure intention must lie behind the spending. The more sound the intentions motivating the heart, the greater the reward will be. Some of the intentions that one may have are obeying Allah, fulfilling a religious obligation, striving for the sake of Allah, satisfying some of the needs of Muslims, empowering people to provide for their families, becoming educated, or getting married, or training the self to fight off greed and reluctance in spending.

1 The Quran, 2:245.
2 The Quran, 4:128.
3 The Quran, 92:17-18.

One should choose only pure, permissible sources of wealth to spend from. Allah is Good and only accepts what is good. Select the most beneficial venues through which to spend your money, according to the priorities of your community.

Do not be impressed by the greatness of the deed you performed, after you have spent for the sake of Allah. This is to encourage yourself to spend again and not to feel that what you have done is sufficient. Keep the deed a secret in order to avoid showing off and receiving praise. Sometimes, spending publicly may encourage others to follow your example. In that case, spending in front of everyone may bring about even more reward if your intention is right. The Prophet⁣ said, "Whoever sets a precedent for good will receive reward for everyone who follows him."[4] He also said,

> Whoever calls to goodness will have the reward of everyone who follows him, without decreasing their reward in the least. And whoever calls to misguidance will be blamed for all who follow him, without decreasing from their own individual blame in the least.[5]

You should not expect something in return for your charity nor should you entertain feelings of patronization. This sense of entitlement will bring the spender only loss, since the reward for his good deeds was canceled by the sins he earned. Allah says in the Quran, ⁣O you who believe! Do not cancel your charity by reminders of your generosity or by injury.⁣[6]

4 Muslim.
5 Muslim.
6 The Quran, 2:264.

Hajj

The Prophetﷺ once said, "The reward for a well-performed Hajj can only be Paradise." A companion asked, "Messenger of Allah, what is a well-performed Hajj?" He answered, "One in which there is only good words and feeding of the needy."[1]

Hajj, like all acts of worship in Islam, is supposed to have a profound effect on the Muslim's heart and actions. The Prophetﷺ set the example of a Hajj that achieves these goals. It is a good idea to study the Prophet's approach to Hajj when you are considering embarking on this life-turning journey.

Every penny that is spent on the Hajj journey should be from permissible money. There should be neither extravagance nor extreme frugality in the arrangements of the pilgrimage. The young Muslim setting out for Hajj must keep in mind that any difficulty she may experience will be for the sake of Allah, and the reward for being patient during the inconveniences of Hajj is worth it.

When arriving at the house of Allah and upon reciting the greeting "*Labbayk Allahuma Labbayk,*"[2] you should recall that you have truly answered the call of Allah. When you witness the massive crowds

---

1 Ahmad.
2 "To You, Allah, I have answered and come."

and oceans of people, think of the Day of Judgment when all humanity will be resurrected and summoned in fear and confusion to stand before its Creator. Think of the equality of every man, woman, and child, as they all wear the same clothes, perform the same acts of worship, and stand shoulder to shoulder. No distinction is made between citizens of different countries, or people of different social and economic backgrounds; the only true distinction is their level of taqwa, which is known only by Allah.

Restrain yourself from all sin, argumentation, and obscenity, as commanded in the Quran. Strive to embody the true Muslim character especially with respect to the rights of other Muslims, bearing their ill behavior and treating them graciously.

Seeking Knowledge

When seeking knowledge, the young Muslim should constantly renew her intention, making sure that her knowledge will elevate her in the sight of Allah. Seeking knowledge can lead to two paths: one through which the seeker increases in improving herself and fearing Allah, and another in which the student becomes conceited and full of herself.

Those who walk on the first path are described in the verse, ﴿Those who truly fear Allah among His Servants are those who have knowledge.﴾[1] The second kind are described in the hadith, "Whoever seeks knowledge in order to compete with the scholars, impress those easily deceived, and elicit the admiration of people will be in Hell."[2]

In order to seek knowledge humbly and properly, the following etiquette should be observed by the seeker of knowledge. She should thoroughly purify and formulate her intention to seek reward from Allah and earn His pleasure. The Prophetﷺ said, "Whoever takes a path seeking knowledge, Allah will ease his passage to Paradise."[3] The student of knowledge should also have the intention of fulfilling

1 The Quran, 35:28.
2 Tirmidhi.
3 Muslim.

her obligation towards the collective community of Muslims all over the world. The Prophet said, "Seeking knowledge is an obligation on every Muslim, male and female."[4] The task of seeking knowledge can either be an obligation on every individual or only on a select few, depending on the context and the field. Certain kinds of knowledge are an obligation on every one of us who have the capability to attain them. We will be rewarded for pursuing this knowledge and punished if we neglect it. For example, learning how to pray, the rulings of purification and prayer, the rulings regarding fasting during Ramadan, the etiquettes and obligations of marriage if one is getting married and the basic knowledge surrounding any obligatory act of worship is a must for every capable Muslim. Similarly, a basic understanding of the principles of the Islamic creed is also essential.

Other kinds of knowledge are not obligatory on each one of us to pursue because if some amongst us are learning in those fields it suffices us all. If none of us are pursuing these types of knowledge, then all of us carry the sin of neglecting the responsibility. These kinds of knowledge include fields such as medicine, environmental sciences, social work, and the Islamic sciences. If we lack experts in any of those fields, the entire Muslim community—and indeed the world—will suffer. However, we do not need every single Muslim to specialize in these fields. Rather, we need a wide variety of expertise and knowledge in every field, in order to fulfill our mission of leading humanity.

The seeker of knowledge should intend to serve humanity in general with her knowledge, including the Muslims specifically. She should not withhold her knowledge from others who would like to

4 Ibn Majah.

learn. The Prophetﷺ said, "Whoever is asked about knowledge and hides it will wear a harness of fire in Hell."[5] The student should always check herself, to make sure she does not think of herself as too important, superior, or deserving of admiration. She should also exert her utmost effort to pursue knowledge with perfection and dedication. She should be keen to increase her knowledge and attain higher accomplishments in her field, while also helping others improve and learn.

---

5 Tirmidhi: hasan.

Remembrance & Contemplation

⟨ Soon will We show them our Signs in the furthest regions of the earth and in their own souls, until it becomes manifest to them that this is the Truth. ⟩ 1

Contemplate the signs of Allah in human beings, the mountains, the forests, the soil under our feet, and the oceans; the breathtaking skies, planets, and stars. This thought and remembrance brings about a deep faith that is unshakable. It can lead us to be profoundly convinced that such great creation is evidence of an even Greater Creator.

Constant remembrance of Allah, His Paradise and reward, and His Hell and punishment will similarly lead to a deep awe and mindfulness of the Creator. Our souls will long for Paradise, fear Allah's anger, and become motivated throughout our life journey of self-improvement. Allah says in the Quran, ⟨And men and women who engage much in Allah's remembrance—for them has Allah prepared forgiveness and a great reward. ⟩ 2

1 The Quran, 41:53.
2 The Quran, 33:35.

Our entire life can be an embodiment of our remembrance of Allah. Prophet Muhammadﷺ showed us how this is possible. He taught us remembrances to say in the morning and in the evening; when we enter our homes and when we leave them; when we eat, drink, dress, and enter the bathroom; when we have intercourse with our spouses; and in all circumstances, whether we are at ease, in difficulty, or seeking repentance after sins.

Every good action we perform, even our 'neutral' daily routine, can be part of this life of continuous remembrance. By having before every action good intentions that revolve around our mission to serve and please Allah, your life will become a life of remembrance. Going out to work everyday, studying for classes, visiting friends, shopping for groceries, and spending time with family all become acts of worship and remembrance if they are preceded with sincere intentions and mindfulness of Allah.

The Best Form of Remembrance
The best form of remembrance is reading and reciting the Quran, the literal revealed words of Allah. The Quran is the constitution and foundation of the Muslim's life. In it are our codes of living, far-reaching principles, practical advice, wise direction, and the pillars of our faith. In it are promises about our future and the consequences of our actions. In it are the values which we must apply in every area of our personal and community life: ❨Surely this Quran guides to that which is most upright.❩[3]

In order for this form of remembrance—the reading and recitation of the Quran—to have the desired impact on our quest for self improvement and closeness to Allah, we should strive to apply the following etiquette towards the Quran. Try to have wudu before recit-

3 The Quran, 17:9.

ing, if you are able. Read in a peaceful environment so that you can fully contemplate the significance of what is before you. Be aware of the greatness of the words and the greatness of Allah, The One who spoke them. Strive to internalize the meaning of what you read. Feel that every sentence is directed towards you as a person.

Allow the Quran to influence your thoughts and feelings. When you read verses of warning, be afraid. When you read verses of forgiveness, feel hopeful. When you read verses of command, rise to action. In order to have this deep level of interaction with the Quran, the Prophetﷺ recommended a slow, contemplative reading of the Quran. He said, "Whoever reads a letter from the book of Allah will have a reward. Each reward is multiplied ten times. I am not saying that Alif, Lam, Meem is a letter, but Alif is a letter, Lam is a letter, and Meem is a letter."[4]

Be consistent in your daily recitation of the Quran, for that is the example of the Prophet. We should strive to read the entire Quran on a periodic basis, whether once every three days, every week, or every month according to your abilities. Do not be of those who are unmindful of the Quran and neglect it as their daily regimen of guidance and reflection.

Try to memorize whatever you can of the Quran, because this will help it to be better incorporated in your life. The Prophetﷺ said,

> It will be said to the companion of the Quran, 'Recite beautifully and meditatively as you used to in the world, for your station in Paradise will be at the last verse you recite.'[5]

4 Tirmidhi: hasan sahih.
5 Tirmidhi: sahih.

Supplication: An Essential Form of Remembrance

⟨ When My servants ask you concerning Me, I am indeed close. I answer the prayer of every supplicant when he calls on Me. ⟩[6]

The Prophetﷺ said, "Dua is the essence of worship."[7] In order for supplication, in Arabic dua, to have a positive effect on the soul, we should try to implement the following etiquette of supplication.

Know for sure that Allah is fully aware of your circumstances and trust that He will deliver you and take care of your needs. Know that Allah is fully capably of answering your supplication; sometimes your dua will be answered immediately and sometimes the response may be delayed for reasons that only Allah in His wisdom knows.

A supplication that is not answered immediately may be a test for His servant or for an unknown benefit. Perhaps Allah has willed out of His mercy to replace the supplication with something else better in this life. Perhaps Allah will delay His response until the Day of Judgment, so that He answers you at the moment when you need it most. The Prophetﷺ said,

> There is not a Muslim on earth who supplicates, except that Allah answers him, stores it for him for a greater good, or keeps an unforeseen evil away from him instead, as long as the supplication does not ask for sin or broken relations." A man asked, "Even if we make abundant supplications?" The Prophet answered, "Allah is more [He will answer more than you can possibly supplicate]".[8]

6 The Quran, 2:186.
7 Tirmidhi: hasan sahih.
8 Tirmidhi: hasan sahih.

Seek out the special times and occasions on which supplication is answered. Some of these times include the last third of the night, when Allah descends to lowest sky and calls out,

> Who is calling upon Me that I may answer him? Who is asking of Me that I may give him? Who is seeking My forgiveness that I may forgive him?[9]

This great exchange happens every night—how fortunate the one who responds with supplication and prayer instead of only unmindful sleep! Other special times include the minutes between the adhan and the iqamah[10], during prostration, when breaking the fast, and any moment when your heart is responsive, fearful, and deeply absorbed in the remembrance of Allah.

The Prophetﷺ observed other etiquette that we should try to practice during our supplication. Turn to face Makkah if you can, raise your hands to the sky, and lower your voice out of reverence and humility. Begin your supplication by praising Allah and sending blessings upon the Prophet. Resolve in your supplication to abandon your sins so that Allah will respond to you. Of course, it is unacceptable to ask Allah for something that is forbidden in Islam; only ask for what is good.

Reduce self-consciousness in your supplication—be yourself! Call on Allah in all sincerity and with your entire being. Do not feel that you must speak formally or memorize long texts that you do not understand. While some find much joy in reciting long, beautiful supplications in Arabic, this should not be seen as a condition for sincere dua. Rather, build a relationship with your Lord in which you can pour out to Him whatever is in your heart. Be less occupied with how you say it and instead concentrate on the spirit of the supplication.

9 Bukhari.
10 The first and second calls to prayer.

Night Prayer

*❴ Their sides forsake their beds of sleep, while they call on their
Lord in fear and hope. ❵* [11]

As with every act of worship, the night prayer should have a profound
impact on self-purification. In order for such an effect to happen,
there are certain recommendations that should be observed. The
first is knowledge. Educate yourself about the merits of the night
prayer. In the night prayer, the slave speaks to her Lord and confides
her worries while everyone else sleeps. She seeks forgiveness while
others are oblivious, and asks her Lord to help her throughout the
day. She begins the following day with a renewed provision of faith, a
glowing face, and a strengthened relationship with her Creator.

There are measures that we can take to make it easier for us to
arise for the night prayer. Sleep early, so that you are well-rested. Observe the sunnah before going to bed: make wudu, lie on your right
side, and recite the recommended supplications before you sleep. If
you are busy with good actions after isha, such as seeking knowledge
or studying, attending a meeting for Islamic work, or spending time
with family, then it is best for you to pray the night prayer before
you sleep. Imam Ash-Shafi'i used to spend part of the night seeking
knowledge and part in prayer, after which he would sleep for the
remainder.

Another measure to encourage performance of the night prayer
is to limit the amount of food you eat before sleeping. There is a saying, "Do not eat too much, lest you drink too much, lest you sleep
too much, lest you lose out on too much." Taking a short nap during
the day will also help your body muster energy at night. Make sure
you go to bed with a firm determined intention to wake up—for

11 The Quran, 32:16.

that willpower will help you when it is difficult to leave the comfort of your bed.

Ask those who are close to you—your spouse, your siblings, your brother in Islam—to pray with you and help you to waken. By inspiring others to pray at night, you will be inspiring yourself. You will also be counted among those who encourage and help others to do good. The Prophetﷺ said, "The one who rises at night, wakens his wife and together they pray two rakah—they will both be written as those who remember Allah frequently."[12]

Avoid sins that can help the shaitan dissuade you from your decision to pray at night. Sufyan Ath-Thawri, a great scholar from the generations succeeding the companions, said that he was unable to wake for the night prayer for five months, due to a sin that he had committed. Frequently remembering the Hereafter will make you eager to pray at night, because you will feel the urgency of preparing for that Ultimate Day.

The Levels of Night Prayer

There are different kinds of night prayer, and all are like fountains of reward, mercy, and forgiveness. Read about these various forms of prayer and adopt whichever you choose, embracing it as a means of purification for yourself. The effects on your soul of standing alone at night before your Creator are indescribable.

The different kinds of night prayer are as follows: 1) to pray for all of the night, 2) to pray for half of the night, 3) to pray one-third of the night, 4) to pray one-sixth of the night, 5) to pray whatever you can. The best of these five kinds of night prayer is to pray one-third of the night, because it is the most moderate and balanced of them all. The Prophetﷺ said,

---

12 Abu Dawud.

The most beloved prayer to Allah is the night prayer of
Prophet Dawud. He used to sleep for half of the night,
pray for one-third, and then sleep for the last sixth.[13]

If you find sometimes that the night prayer is too difficult, then you
should not allow its treasures to escape you completely. At least spend
some of the night sitting and remembering Allah by praising Him,
thanking Him, saying La ilaha illah Allah, and seeking repentance.
You can use those moments of the night to supplicate to Allah, read
Quran, and repent. Every minute you spend this way is valuable.

When you go to sleep late, or if you are afraid that you will not be
able to wake up in the last third of the night, then you should pray
your night prayer before sleep. In fact, any good action that you do
before sleep, such as seeking knowledge, helping a friend, or doing
Islamic work, can be performed with the intention of spending the
night in worship. As for the young Muslim who truly intended to
wake up for the night prayer but was overtaken by sleep, his sleep is a
gift from Allah. His reward, because of the sincere intention, will be
recorded. He should then try to make up his missed prayer during
the day.

The Muslim who has made it a habit to pray the night prayer on
a regular basis should beware of abandoning the habit. It is as if this
person had a flowing source of reward and mercy and then deliberately cut off that source. The Prophet once told a companion, "Do
not be like so and so. He used to pray the night prayer, and then
stopped."[14]

---

13 Bukhari and Muslim.
14 Bukhari and Muslim.

Contemplating Death

Contemplation of death and thinking about your future in the next life is a powerful means of softening the heart and growing closer to Allah. Death is so surely in our future that we might as well consider it as our past. Remember the day when you will be lifeless and dead. The earth will be your bed, worms will feed on your body, and either Paradise or Hell will be your future abode.

The Prophetﷺ said, "Increase your remembrance of the Eliminator of Pleasures [death]."[1] He also said, "Be in this life as a stranger, or a passerby." Ibn Umar, a companion of the Prophet, once advised, "If it is the evening, do not trust that you will reach the morning. And if it is the morning, do not trust that you will reach the night. Take advantage of your health for the day you become sick, and take advantage of your life for the day you will die."[2]

If remembering death leads to depression, despair, or apathy, then your approach to this tool of self-purification is incorrect. We should not give up on the world as lost and miserable, just because our time here is limited. Instead, our attitude in remembering death should be to take from this life what will help us in obeying Allah, better

1 Tirmidhi: hasan.
2 Bukhari.

the condition of the world around us, and fulfill our mission as vice-gerents on this earth. In comparing this world to the Hereafter, we know that there is no comparison—nothing is worth pursuing here except what will help us earn the pleasure of Allah.

Contemplating death should help us to be quick in seeking repentance and energetic in performing good deeds, for we know that death can strike at any instant. We are all equally vulnerable to death—it hits those who are old, young, healthy, sick, male, and female. The Prophet said,

> Take advantage of five before five—your youth before old age, your health before illness, your wealth before poverty, your free time before becoming busy, and your life before your death.[3]

The Prophet also said, "Two blessings, which most people take lightly [until they are lost], are health and free time."[4]

The Prophet once warned us of the consequences of taking death lightly. "One day, nations will overpower you as if feasting around a plate," he said.

"Will it be because we are few in number, Messenger of Allah?"

"No," He replied. "You will be many, but you will be like the foam on the sea. Feebleness will have descended upon you."

"What will this feebleness be a result of, Messenger of Allah?" asked the companions.

"Love of this world and dread of death."[5]

---

3 Ibn Abi-Dunya: Hasan.
4 Bukhari.
5 Abu Dawud.

Calling to Allah & Striving in His Cause

Let there arise out of you a band of people inviting to all that is good, enjoining what is right, and forbidding what is wrong. They are the ones to attain felicity.[1]

And whoever strives hard, he strives only for his own soul.[2]

Allah has purchased of the believers their lives and their wealth—for them in return is Paradise[3]

Calling to what is good will encourage the soul in its quest for purification. Jihad, striving for the sake of Allah, frees the soul from the suffocation of worldly attachment and reckless desire. Instead, our eyes are raised towards the higher goal of the Hereafter and improving the human condition for the sake of Allah. The young Muslim who walks this path of inviting to Allah[4] and striving can hope to be accepted as a martyr for the sake of Allah, for he dedicated his life to

1 The Quran, 3:104.
2 The Quran, 29: 6.
3 The Quran, 9:111.
4 *Dawah.*

the service of Allah and the fulfillment of his mission on earth. This is the greatest level of purification that any soul can aim for.

The Prophet۝ said, "On the Day of Judgment, there will be nothing heavier on the scale of the believer than good character."[5] For the young Muslim who has succeeded in abandoning many of his immoral habits and replacing them with well-grounded character and worship: glad tidings! — that is a sign of one who is walking the right path. This young Muslim is living his life to serve his Creator, practice his faith, and call others to goodness and success. This soul is what Allah describes in the Quran as the soul that is truly at peace.

But O Soul at peace! Come back to your Lord, well-pleased and well-pleasing unto Him. Enter among My servants, and enter into My garden.[6]

5 Ahmad.
6 The Quran, 89:27-30.

Afterword

The Role of Tarbiyah in MAS

Before we define MAS as a towering institution with departments, thousands of members, and tens of chapters, the Muslim American Society (MAS) is an Islamic American movement of committed individuals who cherish the divine guidance of Islam as their platform for development, societal engagement, and uplifting reform. In response to the divine call and in pursuit of the greater good, MAS aspires to embody the comprehensive message of Islam and advocate its values.

That lofty mission embodies the model of our beloved Messenger Muhammadﷺ. MAS emulates his example in the United States through discourse and methodical implementation of plans and programs that are relevant to our human experience in American society. The eternal truths of the Prophet's mission are constant and timeless—the fundamental essence of the divine call to change oneself, pursue noble character, and work for the pleasure of the Almighty remains the primary methodology of our mission today. These truths are still the very same ways we can magnificently alter the state of the world around us, starting from within ourselves, our own families, our communities, and lastly our society at-large.

We believe the message of Islam to be the message that befits the innate nature of the human being. It is a message of worship that is conducive to perfecting the human condition. It is a message of the mind that is guided by the Divine, a message of knowledge that is guided by faith, a message of faith that is connected to righteous action, and a message of action that is connected to a compelling sense of mission. Islam teaches that worldly pursuit can be linked to eternal salvation, that the body is in unison with a spirit, that Godly prescriptions are designed to yield human success, and that justice, freedom, and equality apply to every human being.

MAS staunchly stands for this message in an American context, and it is that message that defines our mission here in America. We in MAS adopt the process of tarbiyah and self-development as the cornerstone of our model, as did the Prophet☝. We seek to prepare members of the highest caliber and utmost levels of moral and spiritual character. This book, Rising Soul, which focuses on the fundamental role of reforming the self, is most vital to the success of all of our work. When you are overwhelmed by the magnitude of our mission, rest assured that if you have done your part and made sure that your pact with the Almighty is healthy and vibrant then we are in the best of shape and we are closer than ever to fulfilling our mission and attaining our objective.

On the other hand, if we falter and lose sight of the central significance of self-reform, we will not be any closer to our goals and aims than other lost souls. Nothing else will matter or alter our state of affairs. It all starts from within — then, and only then, will our plans, organizing, members, departments, and implemented strategies and methods become effective tools of societal engagement and uplifting reform.

I pray to Allah (swt) to bless all of us with an enlightened heart, a remembering tongue, a present mind, a repenting soul and a patient spirit. I pray to Allah to guide our steps towards a reformed self that seeks refuge in Him — a self that sees with the brilliance of the Exalted and lives with the knowledge and remembrance of the Almighty.

Dr. Esam Omeish
President, Muslim American Society
October 2006

Translator's Note

2ⁿᵈ Edition

Many individuals helped make this MAS Youth publication a reality—may Allah reward them abundantly and continue to use them in His service. Rising Soul was produced with the permission of Dr. Muhammad Mansur, the author of the original Arabic *Al-Mukhtasar Al-Mufid fi Tarbiyat An-Nafs:* A Brief Guide to Self-Development.

This is an adapted translation, which means that we attempted to adapt the original Arabic text to be highly relevant to an American context. Some verses and *ahadith* were translated in a manner that we hope best captured the meaning of the text, instead of a strictly literal rendition of the words.

The use of Arabic words in the translation was limited to instances in which there was either no English equivalent or the English explanation was lengthy. In such cases, we used the Arabic term for convenience. The comprehensive glossary at the end of the book will help readers who are unfamiliar with the Arabic terminology.

In Arabic, the pronoun 'he' often refers to both genders. In an effort to convey that meaning in English, the text regularly alternates the use of 'he' and 'she.'

This second edition was carefully edited and improved by several editing teams. We ask Allah to accept from all who worked on this project and we beg Him to forgive our mistakes and shortcomings.

MAS Youth Translation & Editing Teams
January 2008

Glossary

Adhan: The call to prayer.

Allah: The Arabic name for God.

Aqiqah: A celebratory occasion upon the birth of a baby in which a sheep or goat is sacrificed and its meat served amongst the people.

Dawah: Dawah literally means an invitation. It refers to the great mission of inviting others to Allah and the religion of Islam.

Dhikr: The remembrance of Allah.

Dua: a supplication: the act of calling upon Allah.

Fatwa: a religious ruling that pertains to a specific situation.

Fitrah: The natural, pure state existing in every human being, which recognizes God and is drawn to Him.

Ghaibah: backbiting or gossip—to say something about your brother in his absence that he would dislike.

Ghuroor: self-deception or a false sense of security.

Hadith: a saying of Prophet Muhammadﷺ. The sayings of Prophet Muhammad were meticulously documented and recorded during and after his death. The plural of *hadith* is *ahadith*.

Hadith Qudsi: A saying of the Prophet in which he conveys something that Allah said.

Hajj: The pilgrimage to Makkah that all Muslims must try to perform at least once in a lifetime.

Haram: something forbidden in Islamic law.

Haya': modesty and wariness due to the presence of Allah.

Hijrah: the Prophet's emigration from the city of Makkah to Madinah.

Ihsan: to perform anything to the absolute best of your ability and purely for Allah.

Ikhlas: sincerity.

Insha'allah: God willing.

Jihad: *Jihad* literally means struggle. Jihad refers to the internal struggle for self-purification as well as the material struggle for justice, peace, and inviting to Islam.

Jinn: One of Allah's creations that were also granted free will and will be held accountable for their actions on the Day of Judgment.

Khushu': concentration and a presence of heart and mind during an act of worship such as prayer.

Madinah: the city to which the Prophet migrated and established the first Muslim community.

Mahram: a male guardian and relative of a woman.

Muhajir: someone who performs hijrah.

Muhasabah: to hold oneself to account and work towards self-improvement.

Mujahid: someone who strives for the sake of Allah.

Muttaqeen: those who have taqwa.

Namimah: slander and defamation with the intention of turning one person against another

Riya': To seek the approval of people or their admiration. *Riya'* can also be translated as hypocrisy, eye-service, showing off.

⬕ : This Arabic notation signifies the phrase *Salla Allahu Alaihi wa sallam*: peace be upon him. Muslims pronounce this phrase whenever the Prophet's name is mentioned.

(swt): abbreviation for "subhanahu wa ta'ala"—most Exalted is He [Allah].

Shaitan: the Arabic name for satan.

Shirk: Associating partners with Allah.

Sunnah: The example set by Prophet Muhammad, which all Muslims must strive to follow.

Surah: a chapter from the Quran.

Tarbiyah: the process of self-purification and self-improvement.

Taqwa: Being God-conscious, God-fearing, and filled with awe and humility before Allah.

Tawakkul: Reliance on Allah.

Tawbah: Repenting to Allah, turning to Him, seeking His forgiveness, and sincerely regretting what has been done.

Ummah: Commonly translated as 'nation', the Muslim *ummah* refers to the collective population of Muslims, across time and space.

Wudu': the prescribed ablution before prayer.

Zakah: a prescribed percentage of a Muslim's wealth that must be given in charity.

Zuhd: worldly detachment coupled with moderation and a balanced understanding.